T. Fowl
5/3/83

THE
POLITICIZED
ECONOMY

THE POLITICIZED ECONOMY

Michael H. Best
University of Massachusetts, Amherst
Department of Economics

William E. Connolly
University of Massachusetts, Amherst
Department of Political Science

D. C. HEATH AND COMPANY

Lexington, Massachusetts   Toronto

Contents

Nature and Its Largest Parasite 103

The Politics of Work 127

The Crisis of the State 159

Preface

Our purpose in this text is to introduce students of political economy and American politics to a radical interpretation of the American system.

The text is introductory, assuming no prior work in political science or economics. It concerns political economy because it probes the political dimension of production, work, exchange, and consumption. We argue that the dislocations created by advanced capitalism cannot be resolved rationally or humanely by the welfare state; the terms of relation between the economy and the state must be redefined. Our disagreements are not only with liberals and conservatives, though. Our emphasis on the political aspect of economic relations and insistence that American capitalism is not the only form a capitalist system can take, place our interpretation at odds with some other radical theories.

Chapter 1 should be read first, and Chapter 6 last. But Chapters 2 through 5, organized around particular issues of public policy, may be read in any order. This format, we believe, makes the text applicable to courses in public policy as well as to more general courses on the American economic system.

Many of the ideas in this study emerged out of two interdisciplinary courses we taught jointly at the University of Massachusetts, Amherst, in 1971 and 1974. We have also benefited immensely from the intellectual life flourishing in the university's Program for Social Thought and Political Economy and especially in the Five College Chapter of the Union for Radical Political Economics. Particularly helpful suggestions and criticisms were offered by Sam Bowles, James Crotty, Kenneth Dolbeare, Rick Edwards, Jean Elshtain, Herb Gintis, Glen Gordon, Jane Humphries, Stephen Resnick, and Robert Paul Wolff. Finally, as this text assumed its final form, we became increasingly aware of the intimate connection between its aspirations and the critical spirit represented by two labor activists of the last generation, Norman E. Best and William T. Connolly. The book is dedicated to them.

Introduction

A text widely held to be unbiased generally reiterates the views of its readers. It reproduces prevailing assumptions without subjecting them to critical scrutiny. We hope that in this sense our text will be thought of as biased and controversial. For in examining inflation, unemployment, inequality, environmental control, the structure of work life, and the crisis of the state, our overriding purpose is to challenge the prevailing accounts of these topics. We do give some attention to the established interpretations. We explore the Keynesian approach to inflation and unemployment, the functionalist theory of inequality, the classic theory of "scientific management" of workers, the market model of environmental management. But our purpose is to expose underlying assumptions that are susceptible to criticism, to show weaknesses in the interpretations, to introduce alternative interpretations that seem to us to account better for the phenomena in question. Although at the moment we will not defend our view of the political economy and public policy—that is a task for the text as a whole—we will specify some of it in advance.

The Politicized Economy

To introduce our thesis, we wish to distinguish first between a simple social relation, a market relation, and a political relation.

An Example: The Marriage Relation

Consider each relation as it might find expression between a husband and wife in a nuclear family. In a simple social relation each partner is connected to the other through a set of traditions unreflectively followed by both. Each accepts an established division of labor and adopts a set of duties and rights attached to that division. If either breaks one of the norms, both agree that an unjustifiable transgression has occurred. The obligations of each, moreover, extend well beyond specific assignments. If one mate should, say, become seriously ill or deformed, the responsibilities of the other are not thereby erased. Love, tradition, and duty are the defining characteristics of this relation.

If the marriage connection were a simple market relation, the obligations of each partner would be quite limited; perhaps they would be specified in a contract. The terms of exchange would not be settled autonomously by the couple, but a competitive market in wives and husbands would establish the going prices. The wife might perform six units of housework in exchange for four units of yardwork. Sexual acts might be classified into types and placed on a preference scale by each partner so that a market rate of exchange could be established. If one partner became ill or ugly, the other would search in the open market for a better deal. Contracts limiting obligations and exchange rates established in a competitive situation would define the market marriage.

Finally, the connection would be political if the parties were interdependent or shared some commitments but were also locked into a continuing struggle over how to constitute aspects of the relation. Perhaps the wife, repudiating the traditional division of labor, would press for a relation in which each would serve as breadwinner and homemaker. Or perhaps the husband, responding to pressures from friends, children, and parents to whom the wife has appealed for support, would adjust the old assignments somewhat but then launch a love affair with a younger person to undermine the confidence and power position of his mate. The possibilities are endless. Struggle and maneuvering within a setting of interdependence, but a setting interpreted rather differently by each party, would mark a politicized marriage.

So far our attention has been fixed on the marriage relation as interpreted by the participants themselves. We have pretended that appearance and reality always mesh in marriage. But it might turn out, certainly, that a power relation actually underlies the market connection, rendering the terms of exchange quite uneven. Or the traditions embedded in the social tie might treat one party as naturally inferior to the other when in fact nothing in the parties themselves requires this treatment. Or the political relation might be informed by aspirations that are in fact unattainable, thereby introducing conflict into a situation for no good reason. When a power relation that is unrecognized by one or both parties distorts a social or market relation, we will say that the relation is partially (or imperfectly) politicized. The relation becomes more fully politicized to the extent that both parties, though generally not in the same way, define it as a conflict over the shape of the relation itself, planning their strategies and responses accordingly.

Relations in the American Economy

With these distinctions in mind we are now ready to summarize some of the points of our thesis.

1. Underlying market transactions in the American economy are power relations that subordinate the worker to the owner, the consumer to the producer, the small producer to the large corporation, and the community interest to private interests. As the adverse effects of uneven economic development, labor mobility, instrumental work, irrational products, unemployment, and inflation accumulate, they unravel the fabric of traditional social relations. And as social ties erode, the power dimension of these relations is magnified.

2. As these consequences accumulate, and the power dimension of market and social relations is explicitly recognized by an increasing number of people, the relations themselves tend to become explicitly and thoroughly politicized. Since the state is the legitimate forum of public accountability, the legitimate arena for resolving public issues, many of these issues reach it, even though they are often redefined by the time they arrive.

3. The welfare state, as the legitimate forum for defining and resolving public issues, is thus the recipient of a proliferating range of conflicts and issues. But, even when humane officials occupy the most important state positions, the welfare state typically lacks the resources to cope with the dislocations of corporate capitalism in a rational or humane way. The very terms of relation between the state and the economy ensure that the system will remain imperfectly politicized in one basic respect: The institution that is legally accountable to the public cannot meet public needs effectively while the private institutions that are not so accountable consistently pursue policies at odds with public needs. In this institutional context the actual responses of the welfare state often sow the seeds of new dislocations. The welfare state is at once a casualty and a catalyst of the crisis gripping the political economy of advanced capitalism in the United States.[1]

4. A properly politicized economy would not be one in which all social relations became political. But it would be one in which the economic and government institutions that shape the life chances of people would come more thoroughly under public control. In a properly politicized economy the privately incorporated economy and the welfare state would give way to the socialist polity. There are dangers and costs in moving in such a direction. But if the interpretation provided here is on the right track, it is the most viable path open to the American political economy today.

Explanation and Prescription

The study of political economy embodies a perspective that American social scientists have sought to avoid, at least until quite recently. Political economists explain in order to arrive at prescriptive judgments. They bridge that artificial split between *is* and *ought* that has led to so much mystification in contemporary social science. We have already disavowed that split, for instance, by suggesting that if our interpretation is correct, the case for a rational exploration of the socialist ideal has been considerably advanced.

Any theory of political economy sets the terms within which prescriptions are formulated and ideals developed. The interpretation contains the ideal within it. It would be strange indeed for someone to accept the free market interpretation of the American system as represented, for instance, by the work of Milton Friedman, and then to opt for socialism as an ideal. For the free market account contains assumptions that, if true, show socialism to be inefficient, coercive, and self-defeating. Socialism simply runs against the grain of human nature as understood by market theorists. It is not by caprice that classical and neoclassical economists celebrate capitalism and condemn socialism: Their own theories make it irrational for them to do otherwise.[2] The task of the student of political economy is to ascertain which assumptions in an interpretation support a particular set of ethical conclusions and then to ask, To what extent are those assumptions justified? How does one decide between these assumptions and other sets embedded in alternative theories?

The assumptions and concepts we employ to comprehend corporate capitalism are most congenial to an ideal of democratic socialism. Where others see disconnected problems susceptible to piecemeal solutions, we see an interlocking set of institutions in need of more radical reconstitution. Where others identify necessary limits set by the dynamics of industrial society per se, we often see unnecessary constraints imposed by the historical arrangements of corporate capitalism. Where they would counsel personal adjustment and collective patience, we would urge impatience and opposition. Our political commitments, like theirs, arise out of our understanding of the established order, and thus it is differences at this level that must be illuminated and debated.

The study of political economy, then, unavoidably connects explanatory theories to evaluative judgments. Because of this inner connection, one who seeks to repudiate a set of economic ideals will be required to undermine the explanatory theory that sustains them.

The Holistic Approach

In identifying structural defects in corporate capitalism, we employ a holistic approach. This approach, unfamiliar to many students of social science, has become familiar to students of ecology. It is the opposite of the reductionist approach, which has been criticized by ecologist Barry Commoner as follows:

> [There is] a specific fault in our system of science . . . which . . . helps to explain the ecological failures of technology. This fault is reductionism, the view that effective understanding of a complex system can be achieved by investigating the properties of its isolated parts. The reductionist methodology . . . is not an effective means of analyzing the vast natural systems that are threatened by degradation. . . . Reduction tends to isolate scientific disciplines from each other and all of them from the real world.[3]

Holists see inner connections where reductionists see separate phenomena. Holists suspect that trying to account for, say, inflation in terms of one or two independent factors wrenches it out of the systemic context in which it is shaped. Reductionists ignore a complex web of internal relations in the name of precision. Finally, holists perceive that interwoven institutions can slowly redefine one another without much noticeable effect and then suddenly generate significant qualitative changes in the entire system.

Ecologists have learned, for instance, that a new parasite introduced into a lake slowly alters the balance between the various species of fish; the new balance increases the vegetation content of the lake, affecting in turn the oxygen content of the water; and these changes together diminish the self-purification capacity of the water. As the changes accumulate, with each accentuating changes in the others, a minor change in the weather, previously without effect on aquatic life, might now kill a whole species of fish. If so, as the dead fish pile up in the water and on the shore, the water becomes more putrid, threatening other species; algae growth flourishes, further reducing the oxygen level in the lake and threatening to kill off all the fish. The relations among the various elements shift, and the system itself undergoes perceptible changes. Reductionists would ask, If the parasite was so important, why did its effects not show up earlier? How come the lake still stinks now that we have eliminated the parasite? Hoping to hold the basic environment constant while experimentally varying specific factors to isolate the causal influence of each, the reductionist misses the point: A new ecological system, quite unlike the one operative when the parasite was introduced, now maintains itself despite the parasite's departure. The whole new system must be understood in order to reestablish the self-purification capacity.

So, too, with political economy. For example, in this text we explore the connections between the instrumental, routinized mode of work that prevails in our society and a variety of other dimensions of the system. The structure of work life, we argue, is internally connected to inequality, environmental degradation, inflation, and irrational product priorities, as well as being an affront to the dignity of the worker. Work life arrangements partly shape and are partly shaped by each of these other institutions, and none of them is adequately comprehended until its connections to the others are understood. Moreover, work routines that were interpreted in one way by workers in an earlier period might take on a different appearance in a later period, even though the structure of the work itself has not noticeably changed. Thus, routinized, authoritarian patterns of work were once legitimated by the promise that they would contribute to the material affluence of future generations. But the future has now arrived. For many Americans, the promise has not been fulfilled, making them cynical about still more promises for a new future. And the progeny of the affluent, having tasted the benefits of affluence, have found it unrewarding. Thus, justifications accepted by an earlier generation become less convincing to a later one. And in the new context, the old modes of work, still required by the system of political economy, generate new obstacles to the smooth operation of that system.

This example merely introduces the methodological principle of this text: Since each institution is interwoven into a larger complex, to understand any one part of the system it is necessary to grasp the whole.

Learning a new theory is like learning a new language: One stumbles at first; constant practice is necessary; long discussions with others similarly involved are indispensable. When journalists, television commentators, educators, and politicians persist in interpreting the issues of political economy through conventional categories, the task is even more difficult. Then it is like learning a foreign language with no one else to talk to and no certainty of ever reaching the country where people do talk that way.

We know of no neat way out of this bind. It afflicts the study of every dissenting interpretation. But since a growing number of people suspect that the established ideas do not adequately explain the established system, we trust our ideas will be given attention. We are not certain that our interpretation is true, but we think it is on the right track. And we know that no one can assess the worth of prevailing ideas without seriously exploring at least one theory that challenges the assumptions hidden inside those established beliefs and ideals.

NOTES

1. Our thesis is thus to be distinguished from alternative interpretations that might look similar at first glance. It differs from (1) the view advanced by some Marxists that the "laws of motion" of capitalism can be comprehended without paying close attention to the politicization of economic relations; (2) the view expressed by many liberals that economic relations are increasingly politicized, but that the welfare state as now constituted possesses the resources to cope humanely with these pressures and problems; (3) the view advanced by classical economists that the state has unwittingly unbalanced self-regulating market relations and that if it would simply retreat once again, these imbalances would gradually iron themselves out.

2. Many social scientists now acknowledge that their biases influence the outcomes of inquiry. Although that is true, it is not the problem we are now addressing. Our point is actually a more basic one: Explanatory theories sustain norms. For development of the pertinent arguments, see Charles Taylor, "Neutrality in Political Science," and William Connolly, "Theoretical Self-Consciousness," both in *Social Structure and Political Theory*, ed. William Connolly and Glen Gordon (Lexington, Mass.: Heath, 1974), pp. 16–66.

3. *The Closing Circle* (New York: Knopf, 1971), pp. 186, 189 (our italics).

Perspectives on Political Economy

Not all perspectives on corporate capitalism in America are equally illuminating. We will examine four models, exemplified in the works of Milton Friedman, Arthur Okun and Paul Samuelson, John Kenneth Galbraith, and André Gorz, and argue that each successive view is an improvement over the preceding one. To set the stage for this examination we must first ask, What is there about the idea of a free market regulating economic transactions that exerts such a powerful grip on so many students of political economy?

The Idea of a Market

The president of Exxon, responding in 1974 to widespread criticism of the high price, low supply, and high profit margin of oil, invoked in the traditional manner the image of the market to ward off "punitive" government policy:

But time and again it has been demonstrated that the free market mechanism

is the most efficient allocator of the nation's resources. The basic laws of supply and demand will bring price into equilibrium and will establish the proper level of production. The consumer is best served by free competition in terms of the lowest price of goods consistent with long term availability. Government attempts to mandate the functioning of the marketplace succeed only in frustrating the efficient distribution of productive resources and products.[1]

Consumers today treat such views of a self-balancing market skeptically. Many believe that such imagery only veils corporate power in the economy and deflects public efforts to render that power more accountable. But since few public officials are willing to replace this old image of the market with a more realistic picture of the American political economy, the image itself continues to prevail by default. It influences our thought and action more than we care to admit. It is, for example, the image of the self-balancing market that sustains the widely held distinction between a *polity* properly subject to democratic control and an *economy* where such public accountability is unnecessary and illegitimate.

The idea of a national market economy is abstracted from the more specific concept of a local marketplace where a large number of independent producers and consumers meet to buy and sell goods. By examining briefly this more specific concept we can, first, derive some of the conditions that must prevail before we can properly transfer the idea from a local setting to the transactions of an entire national economy and, second, come to understand why the image of the self-balancing market continues to be so attractive.

Consider a hypothetical community of family farms situated, say, in the lush plains of Illinois at some time well before 1900. Each family raises crops and livestock, partly for its own subsistence and partly to sell to others for cash. Most of the cattle are shipped to Chicago, but a portion of the farmer's vegetables, fruit, eggs, chickens, and milk is offered for sale at the local farmers' market. Each farmer comes every Saturday during the harvest season to sell some goods and to buy others. Other members of the community (the blacksmith, minister, barkeeper, sheriff, banker, schoolteacher, and so on) also come to the market to buy goods.

We can reasonably assume that each individual will arrive with a solid idea of what he or she needs; with the intention to sell at the highest available price or buy at the lowest available price; with some awareness of the cost involved for other farmers in producing this year's crop; and with a knowledge of the range of prices and product quality in the local market. Finally, most of the buyers and sellers are permanent residents of the community. Their self-respect depends on their neighbors' and friends' respect for them, so dishonest practices like false representation, collusion, sabotage of competitors' crops, and bribery of the sheriff or banker are minimized in this market. The farmers' market, though competitive, is situated within a community characterized by persisting ties of mutual knowledge, trust, and respect.

When such conditions prevail, the market clearly produces benefits for each of its participants and for the community as a whole. The sellers are usually able to get a price that covers slightly more than their costs of production. The buyers are able to compare competing products for quality and price, purchasing those they need at the lowest available prices. The price for any product itself reflects the choices made by the multitude of individual buyers and sellers. And sellers are both encouraged by profits to produce more crops for sale next year and informed by this year's sales as to which items are most likely to be in greatest demand then. The market thus allocates goods efficiently. It also allows individuals freedom to choose among competing goods and sellers. And it does all this without having to draw upon any central authority with sufficient coercive power to set product quotas, determine prices, establish wage levels, or ration goods. Since the need for a central authority is minimal—it enforces contracts and punishes criminals—there is very little chance that the local government will acquire enough power to tyrannize the community. Limited power is not open to corruption to the degree that unlimited power is.

We can now understand why the idea of a private enterprise, market economy is so attractive to libertarians who seek above all to protect the liberty of each individual to own, work, sell, buy, and speak without fear of sanctions imposed by a central power. Such libertarians will find it comforting to view a complex national economy as a market system. But they may overlook features of the larger system that do not fit neatly within the frame of a market system, and thus their policy prescriptions could intensify rather than relieve dislocations in the national economy.

A compelling image, then, can sharpen perception in some settings and distort it in others. But which effect does the market image produce today? This is exactly the question that proponents and critics of market theory of political economy answer differently. To extend the market beyond the boundaries of a local community to the parameters of a nation-state is, in the eyes of classical liberals, to expand the area where economic efficiency and individual liberty can flourish with minimal threat of governmental tyranny. According to critics, though, such an extension must fail: It creates coercive relations between owners and workers; it blinds market economists to those inefficiencies and exploitative tendencies that do not fit into their model; and it encourages public policies that neglect the most pressing needs of subordinate groups. Just as, in an earlier age, social control over mature citizens was sometimes seen as if it were merely a form of parental authority over children so, critics claim, the attempt to treat the national economy as if it were merely a large local market wrongly legitimizes a system of exploitative production and unjust distribution.

The Market Theory of Political Economy

Perhaps the most persuasive and uncompromising attempt to apply the market image to the political economy of contemporary America is found in the work of Milton Friedman. Friedman has led the attack against those who contend that the Great Depression demonstrated the need for massive state intervention into the economy. We can state in summary form the preconditions that Friedman assumes are present in the American system, preconditions that provide the foundation for a viable market system:

1. In each product area there are enough privately owned firms to ensure that no single firm can set prices or otherwise subvert impersonal market controls; as a result prices reflect the pressures of market competition.

2. Barriers to entry, such as capital requirements, economies of scale, one firm's monopoly over key natural resources or distribution channels, are not so great as to prohibit the entry of new firms into the market. Prospective price rises induced by barriers to entry into any specific product line are limited by competition from substitute products (for instance, coal for oil).

3. While each producer seeks to maximize profits within the limits of market constraints, each consumer seeks to maximize private satisfaction through market purchases.

4. Consumers have sufficient knowledge about the quality and durability of available products, the authority of competing advertising claims, price differentials among comparable products, and the relative dependability of firms with respect to

servicing products to enable them to make rational consumption choices within the marketplace.

5. Owners, workers, and consumers sufficiently support market principles and outcomes (the structure of work, nature of products available, distribution of wealth and income) to allow market mechanisms to function with a minimum of resistance and subversion. Mutual consent to most market transactions lubricates the system and minimizes the necessary support role of the state in enforcing contracts and maintaining law and order.

Point 5 is an implicit requirement of Friedman's theory; the others are explicitly avowed in his major study, *Capitalism and Freedom*.[2]

According to this theory, when the preconditions of private property and market competition are met, several benefits emerge: The parties to commodity and employment contracts are "effectively free to enter or not to enter into any particular exchange, so that every transaction is strictly voluntary."[3] Consumers are free to choose among products and sellers; sellers are free to choose which product markets to enter; and the potential "employee is protected from coercion by the employer because of other employers for whom he can work."[4] The market thus coordinates transactions while it protects individuals against undue coercion by other individuals or organizations.

The market economy, which promotes freedom in economic transactions, also provides the necessary condition for political freedom in the modern state. The market, first, removes the need for direct government intervention into economic arrangements; second, it provides the base from which many autonomous and distinct interest groups can emerge to ensure the "dispersal and distribution" of government power; third, it provides relatively secure places of employment beyond the reach of government authority for political dissidents; and fourth, it enables "patrons" with market resources to finance unpopular political programs and ideas. Indeed, the market system helps to ensure that diverse political and economic ideas will be disseminated, for if the demand for radical ideas is high, competitive publishers will strive to produce a supply.[5]

Friedman's contrast model—the system against which he compares the operation of the market economy—is the form of coercive state socialism generally associated with the Soviet Union. This selection is no coincidence, for Friedman believes that any form of collective control over the means of production must destroy the preconditions for individual economic choice and political freedom. The point, then, is not that individuals are perfectly free in a market system, but that they are tolerably free in the areas that count in comparison with individuals living under any other system. Many idealistic socialists, Friedman acknowledges, have said that socialism can promote freedom and equality, but "none of the people who have been in favor of socialism and also in favor of freedom have . . . made even a respectable attempt at developing the institutional arrangements that would permit freedom under socialism."[6]

There are, Friedman concedes, coercive pressures in contemporary American capitalism, but these threats do not come from within the market system itself. They flow out of government intervention into the self-balancing market. The government typically seeks to implement economic "reforms" through public policy, but its intervention invariably undermines individual freedoms while creating economic effects quite at odds with those intended.

Thus, minimum wage laws, designed to shore up the income of wage earners at the bottom end of the scale, actually force employers to lay off workers earning less than the minimum wage, thereby worsening the plight of such marginal employees. Public housing programs designed to improve living conditions of the poor lead to the destruction of many old housing units, to a rise in the number of occupants per dwelling, and to a number of negative side effects associated with subsidized housing. Thus the lives of most of the poor are made worse while urban property and business interests benefit by the removal of poor people and slum housing from the urban core. The graduated income tax, designed to reduce income inequality, encourages the reinvestment of corporate earnings (as opposed to paying dividends taxable at a high rate to stockholders), which favors the growth of the large corporation over the development of new, competitive enterprises. The income tax also generates a huge government bureaucracy to monitor tax returns and to catch those who would evade payments they find unjust. Similarly, the capital gains tax, set lower than the income tax to foster investment, actually channels investment into the largest corporations by encouraging them to reinvest retained earnings rather than distribute earnings to stockholders as dividends taxable at a higher rate. This tax policy reduces the efficiency of the economic system by fostering a concentration of investment funds in established firms.

Friedman supplies other examples, but there is an inner logic that unites most of them:

The central defect of these measures is that they seek through government to force people to act against their own immediate interest in order to support a supposedly general interest. These measures are therefore countered by one of the strongest and most creative forces known to man—the attempt by millions of individuals to promote their own interest, to live lives by their own values.[7]

His conclusion is quite clear. Government must increasingly withdraw from economic life so that the self-balancing market system can reassert itself. And this will only occur if more people come to understand Friedman's theory of the market and his analysis of how government intervention systematically distorts and disrupts the market system. A reduction of its economic activities would allow government to return to its proper functions: defense of the nation, maintenance of law and order, enforcement of contracts, and provision of a stable monetary framework for market transactions.[8]

The most challenging critiques of Friedman's theory of political economy will emerge later as we explore alternative theories, but perhaps some preliminary points can be raised now.

Friedman labels himself a positivist who believes, among other things, that each concept in a scientific theory should be defined precisely and that the conditions of its use should be spelled out carefully so that any investigator can tell when the concept may be used in describing and explaining the economic world. But the idea of freedom, even though it serves as the keystone of Friedman's theory, is nowhere carefully defined by him, nor are we given impersonal means of deciding when it may be applied to economic or political relations. Despite Friedman's casual treatment of the idea it is in fact a controversial notion: Fundamental differences in political philosophy are reflected in differences in the ways it is understood.[9] It is thus not enough to say that "political freedom means the absence of coercion of a man by his fellow men,"[10] because we must first find out what coercion means to the theorist and whether his meaning sufficiently covers the pertinent area. For instance, does the failure to act to eliminate poverty, when such public action is possible, constitute a restraint on the freedom of the poor? Does failure to act when I am in a position to help another constitute a restraint on his freedom? How do these judgments about the meaning of freedom square with Friedman's view that the market promotes, while the government restricts, economic freedom?

Moreover, different ideals of freedom are linked to different conceptions of human nature—why people behave as they do and what is most fulfilling to them. But Friedman does not really confront these issues either. For example, he equates the ability of the consumer to choose between alternative products with the ability of the wage earner to choose a job from those offered by alternative employers. In each case, he says, the consumer and the worker are free from coercion because there are alternatives available. But a socialist, with a quite different view of human nature, would never equate these two choices. For although the worker is (sometimes) free from coercion by one employer because he can work for another, the market system makes him unfree to get a fulfilling job in which he is not subject to the authority of the employer alone but participates with other workers in shaping the conditions of work. For the socialist the private enterprise, market system can itself be coercive in the way it restricts the range of work alternatives for those who do not own productive resources. The socialist will draw a sharp line between owners and workers because, he thinks, owners systematically limit the freedom of workers.

Moreover, even if one accepts his idea of freedom and his view of human motivation, an internal defect of some importance in Friedman's theory, renders his ideal of the self-balancing market utopian in the sense that, by his own assumptions, no political system can be devised that would both protect freedom and minimize state intervention in the market economy over the long run. That is our charge. Let's see if it can be sustained.

Short-term government intervention in the market, in Friedman's view, is systematically counterproductive. Why, then, does the government intervene? Is its intervention endemic to market capitalism and democratic government, or is it simply the result of bad policy decisions by unintelligent liberals in office? Friedman does not say. Rather than analyzing the causes of intervention, he simply casts blame on the government for its action. For example, explaining the government's recurrent temptation to introduce wage and price regulations as part of its effort to hide its own responsibility for inflation, he says: "Governments ask for the self-restraint of business and labor because of their inability to manage their own affairs."[11] But this avoids rather than answers the important question: Why are governments unable to manage their own affairs?

Let us examine a bit more closely the view of political activity and government decision making implied by Friedman's market theory of economic transactions. One important virtue of the market is that it provides the economic base from which a variety of interest groups can organize and press their claims upon government. And we can expect each group that is able to organize to do so because its members will want to mobilize political resources to protect or advance interests they share. The market theory of the economy implies, in short, a *pluralist* theory of the polity, in which many groups advance their claims upon government, each group receiving some of what it wants and no group receiving everything. The pluralist image of democratic politics is in fact very much like the market image of economic transactions.[12]

Suppose under these general conditions a company gains a temporary market advantage; perhaps a key resource of its competitors is depleted, or its own managers are more efficient, or it gains a lucrative government defense contract. We must expect the company to seek to consolidate its temporary advantage; and one likely way is by seeking to influence government policy in its favor. It will convert part of its economic advantage into political resources (contributing to key congressional campaigns, bribing officials, promising bureaucrats future jobs in its company, and so on) and then use those resources to gain policies that shore up its market position (for instance, favorable tariffs, long-term government contracts, access to inside information on diplomatic initiatives, credit policies, highway programs). In this way it may well convert its temporary advantage into a permanent position of market superiority. And this behavior would be quite rational, according to Friedman's, because it promotes the firm's self-interest.

Similarly, we can expect that if a large number of citizens are jointly disadvantaged by market processes, they will use their voting power to influence public policy in their favor. They might seek unemployment compensation, public health insurance, social security, and so on to relieve pressures and risks imposed by the market. To press in such directions might be irrational (given Friedman's assumptions) from the vantage point of the long-range public interest, but it is quite rational from the vantage point of the short-term private interest of those who suffer losses from the market system.

Now, it is demonstrably easier in a pluralist democracy for a group to secure a public policy to its advantage than it is for other groups to reverse that policy once its wider disadvantages become clear. For the group intensely committed to the prevailing policy usually has to defeat counterproposals at only one point in the complex legislative-executive-bureaucratic process, while the more diffuse opposition must be successful at every stage in order to get its policy through. Thus we can see that the continuing pressure of each group to manipulate the market in its favor accumulates into a pattern of government intervention into the market. The predictable result is a large set of policies supporting the most powerful corporations and a smaller pile of welfare policies supporting citizens trying to protect themselves against unemployment, indigency in old age, high medical costs, and so on.

If these tendencies are, according to Friedman's assumptions, built into the very pattern of interaction between a private market economy and a pluralist polity, how could he seek to forestall them? He might opt for limitations on the freedom of groups to organize and to press for public policies that would give them a short-run advantage. But Friedman could hardly accept this response. It would undercut his basic justification for the market system itself. For that justification rests on the claim that the market system, more than any other system, protects the freedom of individuals to organize and to press claims upon the government.

Another response, more congenial to Friedman's orientation, is to persuade private citizens, business managers, and government officials that continued intervention in the market system is against the public interest in the long run, however tempting it might be to particular interests in the short run. This is the note upon which Friedman ends *Capitalism and Freedom*. We must warn citizens, he asserts, of "the threat that we face"; and we can only hope to reverse established trends "if we persuade our fellow men that free institutions offer a surer, if perhaps at times a slower, route to the ends they seek than the coercive power of the state."[13]

But given Friedman's assumptions about the springs of human behavior when people are free, we must expect his plea to be accepted by many groups rhetorically, only to be ignored when each group pursues its self-interest through government. Friedman has accounted for the failure of government intervention, remember, on the grounds that it seeks to persuade people to forgo their immediate interests in the name of the public interest. But his own call to restrain government intervention into the economy falls into the same trap. It calls upon people "to act against their own immediate interests" by refusing to seek market advantages through government policy "in order to promote a supposedly general interest"— maintenance of the market system.

When its political and economic tendencies are explored in conjunction with Friedman's assumptions, the system of market capitalism and pluralist politics emerges as an inherently unstable system. It tends to evolve into the very corporate capitalism and welfare state that Friedman decries. Only if he were ready to give up a key premise of his theory would this undesired implication be avoided. But if he were to drop the premise that only a system in which people are free to follow their short-run self-interests can operate noncoercively and effectively, one of the central reasons for adopting the theory in the first place would disappear. His failure to confront these issues results, we think, from a tendency in classical and neoclassical economic theory that the perspective of political economy seeks to avoid: the failure to explore carefully the dialectical relation between economic transactions and political practices.[14]

The Mixed Economy in the Welfare State

The main body of contemporary economic thought, neoclassical theory, treats the economy as a mixed system in which, as Paul Samuelson expresses it, "both public and private institutions exercise economic control."[15]

In many areas of the economy, such as agricultural production and service industries, the market rather efficiently regulates wages, prices, and production levels in the interests of consumers. In other areas, such as steel and automobile production, a few producers dominate the market; together constituting an oligopoly, they exercise some control over prices. In a very few areas, such as telephone and electric utilities, one producer dominates the market. In the last two sectors large, highly capitalized firms are efficient in fulfilling consumer demand, but the controlling firms' large share of the market requires that the government intervene to some degree in order to compensate for reduced influence of the market. According to neoclassical theory, then, the government should and does operate as a regulator of monopolies, an enforcer of antitrust laws against oligopolistic firms possessing discretionary market power, a provider of public funds where market competition and government regulation place certain groups at serious disadvantage or fail to fulfill important needs of the entire population; and a stabilizer of the business cycle through fiscal policies (such as rates of taxation and levels of government expenditure) and monetary policies (such as adjusting the supply of money) to sustain growth without high inflation, high unemployment, or balance-of-payment difficulties.

In this revisionist theory government plays a crucial role in the economy. If the system is to work equitably, government must often intervene for particular disadvantaged groups (members of depressed areas, victims of discrimination, the elderly) and collective interests not adequately protected by the private economy (pollution control, education, defense). It is therefore absolutely essential that the government itself be responsive to democratic controls. The mixed economy, in short, requires the politics of democratic pluralism, where public elections keep the state accountable to the people and strong lobbying by private interests shortchanged by the market generates the needed government response.

Neoclassical political economists are generally optimistic about the extent to which the state can meet these conditions. Thus Samuelson, in the first reference to government intervention found in his classic text, says that "the citizenry, through their government, step in with expenditures to supplement the real or money income of some individuals . . ."[16] providing, for instance, old age insurance and hospital beds. But to emphasize that there are properly limits to government intervention he, like Friedman, states that "public benefits through taxes are more coercive than private purchases in the market."[17] Where possible, the market should be left to itself.

During the early and middle 1960s the theorists of the mixed economy were generally euphoric: Their theory seemed to have high predictive power; it was increasingly accepted by the Congress, Presidents Kennedy and Johnson, and the public, and policies based on it promoted growth with high levels of employment and modest inflation. But even before the later increases in unemployment and inflation (an unexpected combination for neoclassicists) critics raised questions that are not easily answered within the confines of the neoclassical model:

1. Why do inequalities in income and wealth, approximately the same today as in 1910, remain so marked in the face of the tendencies toward equality inherent in "natural market forces" and tax policies and welfare programs designed to narrow them?

2. Why does the system of production for private profits produce such disastrous effects on the environment, threatening the clean air, pure water, plentiful minerals, and fertile soil that sustain human life and economic productivity?

3. Why does discrimination persist between white and black, men and women, in spite of competitive forces that should presumably reward the nondiscriminating, lower-cost firms with higher profits and threaten the discriminating, higher-cost firms with market failure?

4. Why do the greatest and most direct benefits of government programs in defense, police service, highways and air terminals,

higher education, research, slum clearance, and housing subsidies flow disproportionately to the most affluent when the ostensible point of the welfare state is public action in support of
the most needy?[18]

5. Why does the mixed economy promote such uneven development, so that large cities face continual crisis while suburban
   areas flourish, the Southwest booms while Appalachia lan-
   guishes, some suffer from malnutrition while others seek new and
   exotic luxury goods?

6. Why does the United States maintain such a huge military and
   intelligence presence in the nonindustrial countries with which it
   trades? Since the imminent threat of Soviet invasion in most of
   those countries is minimal, is there some connection between
   our system of political economy and the United States international militarist posture?

7. Why do so many of the children of affluent parents, who have
   experienced at first hand the benefits of consumption, demonstrate in one way or another that they take little comfort in the
   opportunities for work and consumption that await them?

To pose these questions is to reveal that while neoclassical
economists have a theory of what motivates consumers and firms
and a view of what role the government ought to play in the
economy, they do not in fact have a developed theory of political
economy. With the exception of questions 1 and 2, which we will
explore later, neoclassical theorists typically ignore these issues or
treat them as if they were "political" or "social" issues somehow
separable from the autonomous system and discipline of economics.[19] They show little awareness in their writings that changes in the
organization of economic life have penetrated into the very structure
of political life and have rendered economic life itself indelibly political.

Arthur M. Okun, chairman of the Council of Economic Advisors
under President Johnson and author of *The Political Economy of
Prosperity*, typifies this perspective.[20] He devotes most of his book to
an exposition of how economic advisors under Kennedy and
Johnson were able to promote prosperity (sustained increase in
aggregative output and income) through the subtle use of tax
policies, selective government expenditures, and regulation of the
money supply. He closes on a plaintive note, maintaining that an
unpopular war generated economic activities and government policy
that disrupted the best-laid plans.

After concluding his analysis of the economics of prosperity Okun acknowledges that even during the peak years of success, the policies supporting prosperity did not make the cities safer or more attractive, or ease industrial pressure on the purification capacities of the air and waterways, or make mass transit available for low-income citizens, or reduce military spending to free funds for other purposes. "In retrospect," he says, "I wish more of the fruits of growth had been devoted to the public sector than to the mere expansion of private affluence."[21]

But why hasn't the public benefited more? Why are current neoclassical recommendations for sustained growth remarkably like those that produced the results Okun now regrets? Why have the public expenditures of the past been more favorable to the wealthy than to the poor? Okun does not pair his expressions of regret with new answers to these pertinent questions. He seems content to assert that today, as yesterday, the policy proposals of the advisor must work within the constraints of a "pluralistic political process" in which organized groups "present their views and press their cases."[22] The key constraint in the political system "is not primarily wealth or class; small businesses are as powerful in this respect as the mighty giants of the petroleum industry."[23] The key, apparently, is that organized interest groups always have an advantage in a pluralist system over the unorganized public interest. Legislators will respond, for example, to the strong pressure from milk producers for a price increase, because while the benefits to the producer will be great the cost to each consumer will be minimal, and the legislator prefers diffused discontent that he can avoid to intense discontent focused upon himself. This is offered as a sufficient analysis of how political constraints can limit the economic advisor's ability to generate rational economic policy.

Okun's failure is this: In office he works as a technician promoting economic growth through policies limited by certain political constraints. Out of office he moralizes over the need for more equitable growth policies but fails to suggest how such policies could be constructed and why they remain outside the range of political dialogue. Operating first as economic technician, then as economic moralist, he never really speaks as a political economist.

The Planning System in the New Industrial State

John Kenneth Galbraith makes an effort to explain phenomena that other economists have taken for granted or treated as being outside of economics. Individual freedom through market competition is the keystone of Friedman's theory, and sustained economic growth through a mix of market and government controls is the core of the Samuelson-Okun position. Understanding and taming the power of the large corporation is the central theme of Galbraith's work.

In an early book, *American Capitalism: The Concept of Countervailing Power*,[24] Galbraith argued that the rapid growth of oligopolies in many product areas rendered the market less and less effective in regulating corporate behavior. The corporation, through its ability to set prices, bargain for wage rates, plow back retained earnings, and locate in the most favorable labor market and political climate, has accumulated great power. But, Galbraith then argued, its power is restrained by countervailing power, by the ability of other large organizations to apply pressure to it when its policies infringe upon their interests. General Motors' power to set wages is limited by the countervailing power of organized labor to strike; its ability to set prices is limited by the bargaining power of other large firms that furnish it with needed materials; its ability to exploit consumers through exorbitant prices or shoddy products is limited by the government, which in turn is responsive to the general population through elections and interest group pressure. In Galbraith's early system the government is an umpire, stepping in to aid those groups and interests that lose out in the system of countervailing power operative in the economy. The entire system of political economy emerges as a delicate set of balances among corporations, labor, and consumers in which no organization gets its way completely and few are left out entirely.[25]

But in his more recent studies, particularly *The New Industrial State* and *Economics and the Public Purpose*,[26] Galbraith has modified his initial theory: Power remains the cornerstone of the system, but the emphasis has shifted to the corporate sector, or as Galbraith describes it, to the planning system.

Galbraith's revised theory consists of a complex set of claims, nicely stated but vaguely formulated. We will summarize his central ideas by considering his views about the economist as apologist, the nature of the planning system, the determinants of consumption, the relations between the planning system and the market system, and the relation between the state and the economic system.

The Economist as Apologist

The market model of economic transactions was initially applied to a system of many small firms competing for consumers in a setting where the barriers to entry for new firms were minimal. Why does the market model still attract academic economists, Galbraith asks, in the radically different conditions of today? First, because the intellectual framework with which a profession is familiar exerts a powerful hold over the minds of its members, even when changed conditions make it less applicable. It provides them with familiar concepts and assumptions to bring to bear on contemporary issues. Second, in the age of technology and technique the simplifying assumptions of the market model provide a base from which mathematical models can be constructed and refined; the form of the model is nicely adapted to the style of thought preferred by contemporary social scientists.[27] Finally, Galbraith suggests, to explain corporate behavior in terms of its power is to invite citizens and governments to try to tame that power, to render it accountable to those affected by it. Since this is true, "perhaps the oldest and certainly the wisest strategy for the exercise of power is to deny that it is possessed."[28] Economists who join the chorus of such denials retain in this way the respect and support of the planning system. They serve, half unwittingly, as the apologists for that system. Habit, adaptation to a preferred style of thought, and self-interest converge in this way to sustain a system of thought that is not supported by the evidence. This is a harsh charge; its validity depends upon the truth of Galbraith's claim that the images projected by market theorists do not fit the new system of political economy.[29]

The Planning System

The planning system, one of two systems that together constitute the American economy, consists of a few hundred of the largest corporations. In 1971, 333 industrial corporations controlled 70 percent of all assets employed in manufacturing; and in transportation, communications, banking, and finance, a similar if less extreme concentration can be discerned.[30] In Galbraith's view, the owners of these large corporations have less and less power over the firms' policies.[31] Control is typically dispersed among a rather large group of managers and technicians in the contemporary corporation, and the owners themselves are less and less able to understand the complexity of the institution that pays them dividends. Power has shifted to the corporate technocracy, to the administrative officers, budget analysts, engineers, and other technicians who work in committees inside the corporate bureaucracy.

That segment of society controlling the factor of production most scarce and most strategic to the production process will invariably play a pivotal role in shaping the economic life of its period. In agricultural society land was the strategic resource; the owners of land were therefore powerful men. Control of capital was a prime source of power in an earlier phase of accumulation in the capitalist system. But today possession of technical, specialized knowledge has become crucial; it is central to the planning system. And those who possess these skills—the technocrats—have therefore become the pivotal power brokers of our age.

Technology involves the application of scientific knowledge to practical tasks. In a large, highly technical productive enterprise several conditions must be met if production and marketing are to proceed smoothly: A large amount of capital must be available; human production assignments must be narrowly and precisely defined; the lead time from the inception of a product idea to the beginning of mass production is necessarily long; specialists in organization and coordination, none of whom can alone understand the entire process in detail, must together plan research, production, marketing, and sales so that the entire operation proceeds coherently. These are the conditions of modern production that make planning imperative.

The technocracy, to plan effectively, needs a reliable source of capital, usually to be found in the retained earnings of the large firm. It must have a reliable work force trained in the production skills needed. It should have some control over the raw materials and primary products it will use in production so that these items will be available in the right amounts at the right prices at the right time. It needs to know that the product it is designing today will be demanded by consumers some years later when the product is finally made. And it must know that the state will continue to pursue policies compatible with its capital, labor, materials, and market requirements. Thus the advanced technology of the modern corporation requires extensive planning, and the planning can be effective only to the extent that the environments inside and outside the corporation are subordinated to the plan. Such reliability is best maintained through technocratic control over those factors. Galbraith clearly believes that these conditions are approximated in the new industrial state:

> But much of our life, and nearly all of it that involves the procurement and use of income, is subject to the decisions of

the technostructure. It sets our prices, persuades us on our purchases, and distributes the resulting income to those who participate in production. [32]

The technocracy, according to Galbraith, is not guided solely by the profit motive. It does seek enough profit to finance expansion and to pay reasonable dividends to nonresident stockholders. But it is primarily concerned with retaining its autonomy in decision making, increasing the size of the corporation it runs, and expanding the frontiers of technological research and its application to production. Fulfilling these objectives enhances the status and prerogatives of the technocracy: New positions are created for more technocrats; their skills become indispensable to the corporation; and outsiders (including owners and government bureaucrats) must rely more and more on the technocrats' judgment to appraise corporate objectives and performance.

But if the technocracy increasingly controls the market instead of being controlled by it, and if it is not motivated simply by higher profits, two basic tenets of classical and neoclassical economic analysis have lost their validity. To what extent, then, is the planning system controlled by or accountable to new forces? Galbraith clearly thinks that the state, organized labor, and the market each exercise some degree of control over the planning system, but he also thinks that the balance has shifted in favor of the planning system itself. It controls much more than it is controlled. As the corporation grows, "the goals of the corporation will be a reflection of the goals of the technostructure. And the goals of the society will tend to be those of the corporation." [33]

The Determinants of Consumption

In the theories considered earlier, the individuals are seen as the authors of their own demand for consumer goods. Those firms survive, in the long run, that serve the desires of autonomous consumers; and if the consumers' desires are sometimes frivolous or if fulfilling them requires the destruction of scarce resources, the pollution of waterways, or sacrifices in the production of public goods such as health care and education, the ultimate fault lies not with the productive system but with the sovereign consumers who impose such demands. Galbraith challenges the doctrine of consumer sovereignty and the tendency of its exponents to exempt the corporate system from responsibility for its production priorities.

Two factors converge to compromise consumer sovereignty. First, the planning system requires a reliable demand for its expanding supply of products; and second, once the system has satisfied the basic needs for food, shelter, and clothing, at least of the affluent, it can rather easily manipulate the less basic desires of the affluent. "The further a man is removed from physical need the more he is open to persuasion—or management—as to what he buys. This is perhaps the most important consequence for economics of increasing affluence."[34]

The firm influences demand through advertising, packaging, and frequent style changes. Advertising is the most important factor, and Galbraith insists that his theory explains what remains a mystery to neoclassicists—why the advertising budget of the corporation is so huge. Increasing consumer demand by linking style changes and exotic designs to happiness and status, the planning system helps to create the conditions for its own expansion. It brings consumers, to some extent, under the control of the plan. And if production priorities of the planning system turn out to be irrational in some respects, if the system produces private affluence for some while public programs in transportation, health, poverty, and environmental purification languish, the fault shifts from the sovereign consumers to the planning system itself. Consumers' awareness of the extent to which their own purchases reflect faulty corporate priorities is a precondition, Galbraith maintains, of their emancipation from corporate control.

The Planning and the Market Systems

Auto, steel, oil, and banking companies are prototype members of the planning system, but there are still 12 million smaller firms that fall outside its orbit. Farmers, small retail establishments, construction firms, small manufacturers, restaurants, and garages constitute the core of the market system. The firms in this system remain responsive to the impersonal regulation of the market.

But they are not subject to market constraints alone; they must operate in an environment also populated by members of the planning system. Corporations in the planning system can set a price for goods they will receive from companies in the market system by going to the lowest bidder. They can respond to the demands of their own workers for higher wages by setting a higher price for their goods, thereby increasing the costs to firms in the market sector. They can gain some control of organized labor in the corporate sector by using the surplus labor in the market sector as a potential replacement for unskilled laborers in the corporate system. In most respects, Galbraith asserts, both employers and employees in the planning system dominate and exploit employers and employees in the market system. This uneven struggle between systems, he says, comes to overshadow the more classic conflict between the owning and working classes in a single market system.

The Role of the State

In *The Affluent Society*, Galbraith argued that the United States was marked by private affluence and public squalor: Public needs such as health care and urban renewal, which could best be met through public expenditures, were subordinated to private expenditures for private consumer goods. But he now holds that the national government, especially the executive branch, accommodates its policies to the needs of the planning system in a more subtle way, which cannot be captured by a crude distinction between private purchases and public expenditures. Public expenditures for the military establishment, space and corporate research, highways and air terminals are oversubscribed, while public expenditures for health care, mass transportation, housing for the poor, and education are undersubscribed. The state, in short, employs its resources to provide services and support for the planning system. Other public needs are left in the lurch. Workers and employers in the market system must go to the Congress for their support, because congressmen from smaller constituencies, where local business is important, are most likely to be responsive to them. But Congress is the place where political debate is the loudest and political power the most dispersed. The identification of the planning system with the executive branch gives it yet another advantage in promoting its objectives. Since the success of its policies are now central to the vitality of the economic system, it is easy to argue that the protection of the national interest by regulatory agencies, foreign policy, monetary and fiscal policies requires most of all the protection of corporate interests. If unemployment is high in the planning system, the government must help to spur the sale of automobiles, even if the predominance of the car itself is a crucial ingredient in the energy crisis.

The giant corporation, then, exercises power directly over consumers and over employees and employers in the market system through its ability to set prices, control costs, and regulate demand. It then indirectly exerts power over these same constituencies as citizens by its ability to secure government policies in line with its priorities. Consumers, market employees, and market entrepreneurs are forced to seek whatever remedies they can through Congress, the weakest branch of the national government. The imbalance between the corporate and market systems is extended in this way through the state's identification with the priorities of the corporate system.

That is, in rough outline, Galbraith's theory. It discards the classical separation between a political system marked by power and an economic system regulated by impersonal markets. It challenges the doctrine of the consumer as the sovereign director of the economic system. It repudiates the view that profit maximization is the overriding objective of the firm. It traces many of the structural defects in the American political economy to the unequal terms of trade between the planning and market systems. And it sees the state as the all-too-willing partner of the planning system, extending rather than rectifying the imbalances created by that system.

We believe that Galbraith's theory represents a notable improvement over the Friedman and the Samuelson-Okun theories of political economy, but several defects and omissions remain. First, in his eagerness to emphasize the role of the technocracy he underestimates the owners of capital as a powerful source of resistance to the socialism he recommends. Second, he views the technocracy as the inevitable beneficiary of a line of technological advances that could not have taken any other form. But there is good reason to believe that the direction American technological development has taken is not the direction all technological development must take. If that is true, then Galbraith's theory of technological determinism would have to be modified, and we would have to ask why the United States pattern of technological development did foster the large private corporation, the minute division of labor, the great dependence of workers, and so on. Third, while moving helpfully beyond the simple theory of consumer sovereignty, he still fails to expose the most basic determinants of consumer choice in the political economy of corporate capitalism. Fourth, Galbraith shares with adherents of the first two theories a tendency to focus on relations of exchange between buyers and sellers of goods and to ignore the relations of production between owners and workers in the work place itself. He has introduced political ideas into the relations of exchange, but it is even more important to show how they enter into the relations of production as well. These four areas of criticism are best explored through a theory of political economy that takes them explicitly into account.

The Politicization of Production Relations

André Gorz, a radical political economist and activist in France, has developed a theory of political economy that reflects the influence of Marx's early writings on alienation. In Marx's view, when work life is repetitive and routinized, when workers have little or no chance to interact creatively with other workers in shaping the productive process, when the product of work serves no important social function attributable to the workers, the workers come to experience themselves as passive, isolated beings naturally subordinated to forces beyond their control. They internalize the judgments others make of them as "workers" and their activities and relationships outside of work tend to duplicate those within work. They take on the very characteristics that classical economists assume to be natural to the wage laborer and the private consumer while feeling deep resentment and dissatisfaction with the form of life they are required to live. Building upon this theory, Gorz contends that alienated work and alienated consumption within the corporate system oppress people in their capacities as workers and consumers while generating a potential base of effective opposition to that oppression.

Consider, first, Gorz's view of the determinants of consumption in the contemporary system. He surely agrees with Galbraith's critique of the image of sovereign consumers. But Galbraith's own explanation of consumption pictures consumers as far more gullible and less rational than they in fact are. More important than advertising, or rather, a factor that allows advertising to make such an impact, is the narrow set of options facing potential consumers. They must choose from a small range of available alternatives in order to satisfy their needs for food, recreation, sociability, transportation, and shelter.

As the automobile becomes society's principal mode of transportation, highway systems are constructed by the state to facilitate its extensive use, housing patterns, manufacturing centers and shopping plazas are organized around the expectation of its use. While the state's support services for the automobile are expanded, those for mass transit are allowed to decline. It does not, in such a setting, take slick advertisers to convince people to buy cars. "The possession of an automobile becomes a basic necessity because the universe is organized in terms of private transportation."[35]

The corporate system organized around private profit creates new consumer needs at the same time it serves established ones. When industrial production pollutes the air, urban dwellers come to equate the need for air with a vacation, air conditioning, or a more expensive home in the suburbs. When people hustled off to the suburbs lack public transportation to visit relatives and friends, the need for social life becomes a need for a second car. When the inequality and unstable employment associated with private enterprise produce high levels of crime, the middle class equates the need for security with the expenditures for private schools, household security, insurance, and expanded police protection to protect life and property under these historically specific conditions. When food packaging, processing, and distribution create tasteless food fortified with potentially dangerous preservatives, consumers identify the need for nutrition with expensive organic foods and natural vitamin pills. In these ways the system of production and distribution itself helps to produce new consumption imperatives. The "sovereign consumer" is then forced to choose among a rather narrow range of options to serve these artificially induced needs.

But a viable theory of political economy must not view people simply as consumers. They are also citizens, students, workers, lovers, and parents, and the lives they live in each of these roles affects their involvement in the others. People are not the ahistorical agents of neoclassical economic theory, but social beings constituted in part by the complex web of relationships into which they enter. If, for instance, my work is debilitating and its pace is controlled by others, if it leaves me with little sense of purpose or fulfillment, if it requires me to relate to others only as functionaries, then during my leisure hours I will seek to escape this oppressive reality. The form of my escape will reflect in part the image of myself formed at work and in part the means of escape available in the system. If private consumption is the main game in town, it is the game I will play. As Gorz puts it, the productive system offers private consumption as the "means of evading this intolerable social reality; and the implementation on a grand scale of these individual means of escape (automobiles, private houses, camping, passive leisure) thereby creates a new anarchic social process, new miseries, inverted priorities, and new alienation."[36]

Many needs are collective. Their fulfillment would involve people in persisting relationships of mutual understanding and reciprocity at work, in neighborhoods, and in larger communities. But if work life lacks such richness, then the production system ostensibly designed to serve human beings in fact meets our material requirements in ways that frustrate our needs. People may adjust to these conditions; we may even construe the conditions themselves as part of the human condition. But that is because we fail to explore the possibility of a work process organized with human needs in mind; a production system that provides collective goods such as public transportation, neighborhood laundry centers, day care centers, recreation areas, health stations, and cooperative stores; and a social system that organizes the production and use of goods so as to foster extended relationships in neighborhoods and communities.

Gorz contends that needed and possible changes in work life, product forms, consumptions patterns, and community relationships could foster a social atmosphere more fulfilling than that we now have. Structural change in these institutions would also relieve some of the pressures on the nuclear family. That embattled institution is today called upon to absorb the pressures and injuries imposed upon it from the outside, while its traditional means of performing its functions are being progressively stripped away.

The Galbraithian interpretation of the technocracy is also defective from the vantage point of this alternative model. The technocracy is not quite the power group Galbraith imagines. Linking power to the most strategic or most indispensable factor of production is questionable. Every factor is indispensable to some degree; the fact that slaves were the most indispensable factor to a slave system certainly did not lodge power in their hands.[37] It is true that technocrats do assume an importance in day-to-day decisions not previously noted by neoclassical economists. But technocrats, taken as individuals, often suffer, if less blatantly, from the alienation that plagues other dependent employees. They are typically overtrained for the work they do, and no amount of tinkering with household hobbies can compensate for the "permanent underemployment of abilities in passive and monotonous work."[38] But their technical training is in another respect too narrow. To retain an active presence in an industrial sector marked by rapid change requires a broad, theoretical training, but the technicians' training is often quite specific and sharply defined. As a result technocrats find that they often depreciate rapidly in the eyes of their employers. Many individual technocrats find that the status and the influence of the technocracy in general touches them only during the prime of their productive lives.

When there is a large supply of technicians, owners can select those who are eager to adapt to their purposes. When the economy is under pressure, "technicians, engineers, student researchers discover that they are wage earners like the others."[39] For technocrats, like other dependent employees, can be laid off when their services are no longer needed.

The technocracy sees itself as mediating between groups of

owners and workers, who each seek to politicize the productive process by struggling over wages, pensions, work rates, and so on. But the technocracy, Gorz insists, falsely believes that these issues can be settled by reference to extrapolitical criteria, by reference to the rational imperatives of productivity and efficient economic growth. It tries to expose both groups to the facts of economic productivity and to gain their mutual consent to these imperatives. But this self-imposed role is largely illusory, says Gorz. The technocracy in fact gears its assessments to the expectations owners have for profit and control. This is to be expected when one group of employees in the industrial sector—the technocrats—strives to "keep a balance between a bourgeoisie which is in power and a working class which is not." Its effort must play mostly "into the hands of the former."[40] Failing to understand that the form technological advance has taken under modern capitalism and the relations of production attached to that form do not represent the only pattern of development possible, the technocracy deceives itself ideologically as it accommodates to the employers. It is in this sense that "depoliticization is the ideology of the technocracy itself."[41] And that ideology justifies the role of the technocracy to itself and to other segments of society.

Gorz also endorses a view of the relation between the state and the corporate system that goes well beyond Galbraith's position. In the short run, corporate capitalists, disagreeing among themselves in many respects, will often find their own priorities at odds with those adopted by the state. For instance, owners would often like to convert public resources funneled into education, health, welfare, and retirement programs into disposable income available for consumers to buy the goods of private producers. And when some or all owners act on these preferences they will often find themselves ranged against the public priorities sanctioned by the democratic state. These differences, in fact, typically dominate the politics of party contests, election campaigns, and legislative struggles.

But the corporate system and the state are allies when the more basic, long-range interests of private capital are taken into consideration. "Precisely what distinguishes neocapitalism from traditional capitalism is that the former recognizes the necessity of the mediating role of the state; its efforts no longer aim at restraining public initiative, but at orienting it for the benefit of monopoly accumulation."[42] Public support for the educational system provides trained manpower for each occupational level in the corporate system. Welfare and unemployment programs moderate the boom and bust cycles plaguing early capitalism and dampen potential militancy within the working class. Defense expenditures provide direct profits for many corporations and the means by which other corporate interests are protected abroad. The expansion of the state's role in the economy is accepted, then, as long as its involvement and expenditures support corporate accumulation and expansion without challenging the system of production for profit.[43]

Gorz, though a socialist, is also more wary of nationalization of the means of production than Galbraith is. To nationalize *before* dependent employees have established a more powerful position within the corporate system may well extend the corporate-state alliance to the disadvantage of the lower class. The prior requirement, Gorz contends, is to improve the workers' power position within the firm itself. By pressing militantly for structural reforms— the kind of reform that reconstitutes power relations and creates resources for new advances at a later date—workers can help to ensure that nationalization, when it comes, will come on terms more congenial to worker interests. By establishing a foothold now they have a better chance to participate in management if and when nationalization occurs.

There is no foolproof strategy for progressive change in the political economy of corporate capitalism. The system's ability to divert, deflect, suppress, and destroy dissident movements is well established. But a socialist strategy that proceeds, so to speak, from the bottom up is most likely to promote the desired momentum. It is also most likely to generate a humane socialism oriented to a less alienating system of work.

Gorz goes well beyond Galbraith's break with neoclassical theory in his interpretation of the determinants of consumption and the relations between the state and the corporate system. He also explores the internal dynamics of the production process itself—an important topic almost completely ignored by Galbraith. In fact, Gorz would argue, Galbraith's failure to confront this last area contributes to the defects in his analysis of other areas.

There are deficiencies and omissions in the Gorz argument as well. Thus while he identifies the ways in which the prevailing system generates needs it does not fulfill, he tends to assume that the system can continue to operate successfully on its own terms. If labor does not challenge it, it will continue along the same track. But the capitalist system is in many ways a fragile system, even without a political challenge from labor. The United States, for instance, is a high energy user; its system of production and consumption is predicated upon a steady flow of oil. If oil-producing nations should cut off that supply, the system would face a severe crisis. There is also the fact of nuclear proliferation and the increasing chance that some Third World country will employ nuclear blackmail against the system it views as its oppressor. These and other conditions make the United States vulnerable to repressive police state reactions to such threats at home and abroad. These circumstances, we will argue, provide an additional case for socialism that complements the affirmative case developed by Gorz. Unless we reorganize our system of production, distribution, and consumption, the established system of political economy may crack in dangerous ways.

Also, when Gorz examines the prospects for worker control and the reorganization of work processes he is thinking of a French work force more firmly anchored in a socialist movement than is any segment of the American work force. While his analysis of worker alienation fits the American situation, his strategic program does not now speak to an active movement in the United States. The relations within the blue-collar work force, moreover, do not parallel those in the French blue-collar force. The United States has an underclass of marginally employed blacks, Puerto Ricans, and Mexicans whose struggle for secure employment and adequate income sometimes brings them into conflict with workers in the corporate sector who seek to protect themselves from a similar plight. This intraclass conflict, not really duplicated in France, introduces a defensive conservative potential into the American working class. It may be possible to moderate these tendencies, but this is just one example of the many differences between the two societies that suggest caution in the application of the Gorz model to the American setting.

These specific limitations of the Gorzian theory are linked to a larger defect: His theory of the state in capitalist society is underdeveloped. He tends to assume that the state can successfully maintain conditions favorable to capitalist accumulation. But it may be that the cumulative effect of necessary state expansion into inflation and employment regulation, public education, public employment, corporate research subsidies, military expenditures, public welfare, and highway programs itself contributes to a crisis of state performance and legitimacy. Gorz believes that the repressive apparatus of the state—its use of police, military, surveillance, tax, and employment powers to intimidate and isolate dissidents—will be unleashed when workers challenge the system of private ownership and profit. But he does not thoroughly probe the possibility that the state's failure to deliver on its own promises for material affluence, full employment, job security, inflation control, and equal opportunity will generate a similar response. Gorz sees the state primarily as the protector of capitalist interests. It is perhaps more realistic to see it as sometimes representing capital and sometimes representing the public's best efforts within the prevailing order to cope with dislocations created by capital. Operating within narrow limits of the permissible, the state's best efforts often inadvertently create new dislocations while responding to established ones.

When that is said, though, we believe that the Gorzian model illuminates features of the American political economy overlooked or obscured by the alternative models considered. Sometimes in conjunction with Galbraith's analysis of the terms of trade between the corporate and market systems, more often on its own, Gorz's model deepens our comprehension of structural deficiencies in the American system. We will employ his work as a touchstone for our own assessment of the issues of unemployment, inflation, inequality, ecology, and work life.

American students are not often exposed to the perspective Gorz represents. Lacking exposure to this framework, they lack an opportunity to appraise its strengths and weaknesses. Gorz thinks that this educational deficiency, too, can be explained:

> The domination of one class over another is not exercised solely by means of political and economic power, but also through its evaluation of the possible and impossible, the future and the past, the useful and the useless, the rational and the irrational, the good and the bad.[44]

If some find the initial charge, with its image of class domination, too stark (compare the impact of this picture to that of the market image), they may nonetheless appreciate the challenge of considering a competing view. The best way to reappraise prevailing ideas is to compare them with a theory that locates the possible and the impossible, the rational and the irrational, differently. Only then can one judge reflectively whether the established interpretation or its alternative identify and explain contemporary problems most effectively.

NOTES

1. M. A. Wright, "The Assault on Private Enterprise." Address to the Twenty-sixth Annual Business Conference, Rutgers University, May 31, 1974.

2. (Chicago: University of Chicago Press, 1962). Point 5 is emphasized by some other economists. See Kenneth Arrow, *The Limits of Organization* (New York: Norton, 1974).

3. Friedman, p. 14.

4. Ibid., pp. 14–15.

5. Ibid., p. 18.

6. Ibid., p. 19.

7. Ibid., p. 200.

8. Ibid., p. 27.

9. See, for example, Isaiah Berlin, "Two Concepts of Liberty" (Oxford: Clarendon Press, 1958); Gerald MacCallum, "Negative and Positive Liberty," in *Contemporary Political Theory*, ed. A. de Crespigny and A. Wertheimer (New York: Atherton Press, 1970); Steven Lukes, *Individualism* (New York: Oxford University Press, 1973); and William E. Connolly, *The Terms of Political Discourse* (Lexington: Heath, 1974), ch. 4.

10. Friedman, p. 15.

11. Ibid., p. 135.

12. One of the important modern formulations of pluralist theory is advanced by an economist: Joseph Schumpeter, *Capitalism, Socialism, and Democracy* (New York: Harper, 1947). For a striking example of the use of economic categories in political explanation, see Anthony Downs, *An Economic Theory of Democracy* (New York: Harper and Row, 1957).

13. Friedman, p. 202.

14. This critique rests on Friedman's own assumptions. Our explanation of the growth and import of corporate capitalism is not identical with this, although some points will be the same.

15. Samuelson, *Economics*, 8th ed. (New York: McGraw-Hill, 1970), p. 37.

16. Ibid., p. 44.

17. Ibid., p. 45.

18. For documentation of these points, see Gerhard Lenski, *Power and Privilege* (New York: McGraw-Hill, 1966), ch. 10, and Michael Harrington, *Socialism* (New York: Bantam Books, 1970), ch. 12. Lenski, a conservative sociologist, estimates that "one third to two thirds of the value of all governmental services redound to the benefit of the most privileged 2 percent" (p. 311).

19. A series of studies that have treated discrimination (question 3) as an economic problem began with Gary Becker, *Economics of Discrimination* (Chicago: University of Chicago Press, 1957). Although it is the classic in its field, it sold less than 2000 copies in its first nine years of publication. The studies generally either fall back on outside sociological and psychological factors or, like Becker's, argue that employers with a "taste for discrimination" pay a tax in the form of higher-cost employees. Thus policies designed to increase competi-

tion would force such employers to abandon their "taste" or be driven out of business. However, the origins of a "taste for discrimination" are not examined. See David M. Gordon, *Theories of Poverty and Underemployment* (Lexington, Mass.: Heath, 1972), and Orley Ashenfelter and Albert Rees (eds.), *Discrimination in Labor Markets* (Princeton, N.J.: Princeton University Press, 1973).

20. (New York: Norton, 1970).
21. Ibid., p. 124.
22. Ibid., p. 7.
23. Ibid., p. 8.
24. (Boston: Houghton Mifflin, 1952).
25. For a more detailed summary and critique of the umpire theory of pluralism, see William E. Connolly, "The Challenge to Pluralist Theory," in *The Bias of Pluralism* (New York: Atherton Press, 1969).
26. (Boston: Houghton Mifflin, 1967 and 1973, respectively).
27. The way in which a style of thought appropriate to some highly successful field (say, mechanistic physics in the nineteenth century) tends to be appropriated uncritically by practitioners in other fields where it may not be so appropriate is explored by Stephen Toulmin, *Foresight and Understanding* (New York: Harper and Row, 1961), ch. 5.
28. Galbraith, *Economics and the Public Purpose*, p. 5.
29. Assuming that Galbraith is right about the discrepancy between image and reality, Thomas Kuhn sheds light on the importance of Galbraith's first explanation—the role of habit. A theory, says Kuhn, consists of a complex set of concepts, assumptions, and methods that reinforce one another. Adherents of any such system have internalized this complex over a long period of time. They cannot shed it like a coat, but it is part of them in a way that facial expressions are part of a personality. To drop the theory would be to lose an important part of oneself. One can't always do that, even though one tries. Thus Kuhn finds it understandable that arguments against old theories are seldom accepted by established practitioners. They can always find some way to save at least a semblance of the old theory. The new argument, if successful, can only take hold among new practitioners who are deciding which of two or more systems to make their own. See *The Structure of Scientific Revolutions* (Chicago: University of Chicago Press, 1962).
30. Galbraith, *Economics and the Public Purpose*, p. 43.
31. The thesis that ownership and control are progressively separated was first advanced in Adolf A. Berle and Gardiner C. Means, *The Modern Corporation and Private Property* (New York: Macmillan, 1932). An updated version of that thesis discussed within the confines of a pluralist theory of power is offered in Berle, *Power Without Property* (New York: Harcourt, Brace and World, 1964).
32. Galbraith, *The New Industrial State*, p. 111.

33. Ibid., p. 161.
34. Ibid., p. 202.
35. Gorz, *A Strategy for Labor*, p. 11.
36. Ibid., p. 67.
37. A thoughtful critique of the assumed connection between indispensability and power is developed in Anthony Giddens, *The Class Structure of Advanced Societies* (New York: Harper and Row, 1973), pp. 177 and 262–263.
38. Gorz, *A Strategy for Labor*, p. 106.
39. Ibid., p. 104.
40. Ibid., p. 127.
41. Ibid., p. 122.
42. Ibid., p. 65.
43. Ibid., p. 66.
44. Gorz, *Socialism and Revolution* (New York: Doubleday, 1973), p. 168.

The Struggle
for Security

Instability and Hard Times

A capitalist economy is inherently unstable, and the instability imposes heavy
burdens on vast numbers of people. During the one hundred years between 1865
and 1965 the United States experienced
twenty-five recessions, periods in which
total production declined for at least six
months (see Figure 2-1). The duration of
these recessions varied greatly, from the
relatively mild slowdown of the 1950s,
running eight to thirteen months, to the
sustained depressions of the 1870s and
1930s. Even in the relatively good times
from 1945 to 1970, unemployment, according to official government count, varied between 2.9 and 6.8 percent of the
labor force.[1] Government statistics, however, notoriously underestimate jobless-
ness. For instance, neither workers who
have quit looking for work nor part-time
workers are counted as unemployed in
these statistics. One study has estimated
conservatively that inclusion of the "dis-

Figure 2-1   Historical Fluctuations of the United States Economy

Source: "American Business Activity from 1790 to Today," by the Cleveland Trust Company.

couraged" worker would expand the rate of unemployment by 40 percent; to correct further for those who work part-time *involuntarily* would increase the rate of unemployment in recent years to approximately 60 percent above the government figures.[2] Adjusting the first quarter, 1975, official figures to take these considerations into account, the same study estimates that the official unemployment rate of 8.9 percent signified an unemployment rate of 13.6 percent, an increase from 8.2 to 13.0 million workers.[3] Furthermore, the actual number of people unemployed at some point during any one year is about three times the average unemployment rate for the year. That is, an average unemployment rate of 9 percent for 1975 indicates that approximately 25 million workers experienced periods of unemployment some time during the year.[4] Clearly the official unemployment figures understate the hard times faced by a large number of Americans when the economy operates below its productive potential.

It is tough to be without a job in America. The official expectation is that the unemployed worker will move from geographical areas or occupations of low demand to those of high demand. Thus between 1870 and 1970 the percentage of Americans living on farms declined from over half to under 5 percent.[5] This migration from the farm to the factory or bureaucracy was a painful, wrenching experience for millions of families. In every generation many small entrepreneurs undergo similar agonies as their businesses fail. Sometimes, though, even migration does not result in a job. The Great Depression was such a time. The voices of people who lived and suffered in the 1930s, captured by Studs Terkel in *Hard Times*, express the human dimensions of unemployment during other periods as well.[6] Time-honored means of livelihood were destroyed. On the farm:

> *The struggles people had to go through are almost unbelievable. A man lived all his life on a given farm, it was taken away from him. One after the other. After the foreclosure, they got a deficiency judgment. Not only did he lose the farm, but it was impossible for him to get out of debt.*

And in mining:

> *1929 was when it hit banking and big business. But we had suffering and starvation long before that. In the early twenties, mines shut down, nothin' for people to live on. Children fainted in school from hunger.*

The loss of work affected the family in many ways. Sometimes the father left:

> *The shame I was feeling. I walked out because I didn't have a job. I said, "I'm goin' out in the world and get me a job." And God help me, I couldn't get anything. I wouldn't let them see me dirty and ragged and I hadn't shaved. I wouldn't send 'em no picture.*

Sometimes, when the father stayed, it wasn't much better:

> *I remember how, after dinner, he'd just lie on the couch in utter despair, night after night, for hours. A man who was interested in music, read all kinds of literature, novels, plays, history, economics and so on—there was this man so knocked out. We were afraid he was going to commit suicide. His close personal friend did take a header out of the fourteenth story.*

Increased unemployment swelled the prisons. Times were bad there, too:

> *More people died during that depression phase than they ever did any other time. It wasn't starvation. They called it malnutrition. . . . They made you lose weight until the doctor got after them and said they have to get at least one meal a day.*

Some gave up:

> *The majority of people were hit and hit hard. They were mentally disturbed, you're bound to know, 'cause they didn't know when the end of all this was comin'. There was a lot of suicides that I know of. From nothin' else but just they couldn't see any hope for a better tomorrow. I absolutely know some who did. Part of 'em were farmers and part of 'em were businessmen, even. They went flat broke and they committed suicide on the strength of it, nothing else.*

Feeding a baby in a family without a breadwinner wasn't easy:

> *I remember in Ainsley that year, in the relief headquarters, a woman had been arguing and arguing to get some milk for her baby. You should have seen the things they were giving babies, instead of milk. I remember seeing them put salt-pork gravy in milk bottles and putting a nipple on, and the baby sucking this salt-pork gravy. A real blue baby, dying of starvation. In house after house, I saw that sort of thing.*

Nor was the return home always pleasant for children of the depression:

> *I got tired of hoboing and went down to see him and my daddy*

was all gray and didn't have no bank account and no Blue Cross. He didn't have nothin', and he worked himself to death. (Weeps). And the white man, he would drive a tractor in there. . . .

Housing conditions were often bad:

I remember all of a sudden we had to move. My father lost his job and we moved into a double garage. The landlord didn't charge us rent for seven years. . . . It was awfully cold when you opened those garage doors. We would sleep with rugs and blankets over the top of us. Dress under the sheets.

And worse:

Here were all these people living in old, rusted out car bodies. I mean that was their home. There were people living in shacks made of orange crates. One family with a whole lot of kids were living in a piano box. This wasn't just a little section, this was maybe ten miles wide and ten miles long.

And for those who had a job it wasn't easy either. In agriculture:

In 1939, I went out as an itinerant farm worker. I got a job cutting asparagus, fifteen cents an hour, as fast as you could move. I remember standing up once to rub my aching back, 'cause you worked in a crouch almost at a running pace, and the straw boss yelling: "See those men standing by the road? They're just waiting to get you fired. If I catch you straightening up once more, one of them will be working and you won't."

Or in industry:

When I went to work in January, we were turning out 232 cars a day. When I was fired, four months later, we were turning out 535. Without any extra help and no increase in pay. It was the famous Ford speed-up.

And even some of the rich had it bad:

October 29, 1929, yeah. A frenzy. I must have gotten calls from a dozen and a half friends who were desperate. In each case,

> *there was no sense in loaning them the money that they would give the broker. Suicides, left and right, made a terrific impression on me, of course. People I knew. It was heartbreaking.*

Yet at the same time people were starving, too much was being produced:

> *He pointed out the great piles of oranges, the piles of lumber laying there idle. . . . They'd put up a rick of oranges and apples, put gasoline over it and set fire to them. Vegetables were being destroyed and everything. Everybody who cried so much later about federal programs destroying little pigs . . . they should have seen what industry was doing at this time. To keep the price up.*

This was perhaps the biggest paradox of the Great Depression: underconsumption side by side with excess production. A theoretical impossibility to the free market economists had become a fact of life to the nation. Certainly in human history it has often been true that even when everyone worked there were not enough goods to go around, but during the American depression so much needed to be done and there were not enough jobs to go around. One question must have been asked a million times: Why were so many unemployed?

The Great Depression: A Revolution in Economic Doctrine

The free market perspective, dominant among economists until the New Economics of the post-World War II period, holds that unemployment is the result of, first, workers choosing leisure over work at prevailing wages (an unemployed person seeking work could always offer her or his services to an employer at a wage below the one already paid by the employer), and second, market interventions by protectionist labor unions and misguided government.[7] It fails to explain why suddenly in one period one of four workers should choose leisure over work. During the Great Depression there were long lines for every job available, labor unions represented less than 7 percent of the labor force, and the government had not yet introduced the New Deal legislation designed to promote full employment. Clearly the classical doctrine hardly explained unemployment during this period. It took the Keynesian theory of unemployment to provide an answer and a policy responsive to the new problems created by this depression.

Heretical economists, notably the Physiocrats and, paradoxically, Thomas Malthus, had often argued that market economies suffer from periodic gluts marked by consumption below business production, unsold inventory buildups, and the resultant loss of jobs. But such "underconsumption" ideas lacked a theoretical base until the writings of John Maynard Keynes in 1936.[8] Keynes argued that employment is determined by *the level of aggregate demand* (composed of consumer purchases for the household, business investments on new plant and equipment, government spending and exports) *relative to productive capacity* (the output potential at full employment of labor and machines). Whenever the level of aggregate demand fell short of productive capacity, unemployment would be the result. The crucial element in Keynesian unemployment theory was the level of investment, which depended upon *expectations* of business people regarding profitable opportunities. As Keynes put it, "The weakness of the inducement to invest has been at all times the key to the economic problem."[9]

The Keynesian model of unemployment is based on the notion that investment and savings have double roles. Investment, one of the two main components of private expenditure, is necessary to ensure high employment. But the very process of investing expands the productive capacity and thereby increases the level of demand required to achieve full employment in the future.

Savings, the release of productive capacity (both labor and capital) from production of consumption goods, create the potential for the expansion of capital goods and thus for economic growth. But savings also establish a necessary condition for a business downturn: underspending. A downturn will occur if the capacity released from consumption is not employed in the production of new productive capacity. Put another way, a downturn will occur anytime savings (a leakage from the expenditure stream) are greater than investment (an injection into the expenditure stream). And even a match between investment and savings can plant the seeds for future problems, for investment increases income, which in turn expands savings and therefore the level of investment required to sustain aggregate demand. In short, whenever investment fails to match savings (and is not offset by government or foreign spending) an economic downturn will follow.

In Keynesian theory full employment in a free market economy without government intervention is a special case. According to the free market perspective, unemployment is the special case. Aggregate demand would always tend to equal productive capacity. If households reduced their expenditures (increased savings), the level of investment would automatically expand to utilize the released productive capacity. The released labor and capital would simply be shifted from producing consumption goods to capital goods. Assuming flexible prices, the adjustment process would operate through the price of borrowing money, that is, the rate of interest: As savings increased, interest would drop; a drop in interest would increase the value of investment goods and induce an expansion in their production. The process by which spending equals productive capacity and investment matches savings was referred to as Say's Law.

Keynes denied Say's Law, or any natural adjustment mechanisms ensuring full employment, and instead emphasized unemployment caused by the weakness in the inducement to invest compared with the propensity to save. He wrote: "The desire of the individual to augment his personal wealth by abstaining from consumption has usually been stronger than the inducement to the entrepreneur to augment the national wealth by employing labor on the construction of durable assets." As put by a follower of Keynes, the essence of the Keynesian revolution was in Keynes's ability "to shift economists from thinking normally in terms of a model of reality in which a dog called *savings* wagged his tail labeled *investment* to thinking in terms of a model in which a dog called *investment* wagged his tail labeled *savings*."[10]

The New Economics based on Keynes's writings undermined two central tenets of the free market perspective and became the basis for the liberal government economic policies of the New Deal and later. It held, first, that inequality is not necessary to ensure a source of savings necessary for capital accumulation and economic growth, and second, that the government must intervene in the marketplace to ensure a level of demand sufficient to employ the nation's labor force fully. The classical defense for inequality—the view that capital accumulation, growth, and employment come from rich people's savings—was replaced by the Keynesian notion that savings can easily result in underspending and are therefore often a barrier to growth and employment. The new view of savings thus created a justification for government spending and progressive taxation. Taxing the rich and subsidizing the poor could stimulate demand, employment, and even profits.

But the implications of Keynesian theory for government intervention in the economy went beyond progressive taxation. Keynesian theory provided a rationale for interventionist government policies in pursuit of the four goals celebrated in every standard economics text: full employment, price stability, economic growth, and a favorable trade balance. These goals are to be pursued by an active government stabilization program composed of taxation, expenditure, and monetary policies. The New Economics promised an end to the business cycle and the birth of a new age of unprecedented prosperity based on ever-continuing economic growth. The riddle of unemployment had been solved, and the techniques for its elimination were now available. The only obstacle, or so it was thought, was the absence of a political will to implement the proper government policies at the right time.

The Age of the Economist

The Eisenhower years witnessed sluggish growth rates and unemployment levels that reached over 6.5 percent in two of the three recessions. With that background the New Economists found it relatively easy to convince President Kennedy that government policies of the 1950s had unnecessarily constrained the actual growth below the productive potential. What the economy needed, they claimed, was a boost in demand through tax cuts and increased expenditures. After a couple of years of political maneuvering, the President and (to a lesser degree) the Congress were convinced; the 1964 tax cut was passed. The results matched the predictions of the New Economists. The lower-tax-induced spending increase propelled a 16.9 percent rise in Gross National Product and a 13.5 percent rise in government tax revenues over the ensuing two years.[11] Such success carried with it a smashing ideological victory for the New Economists. They were optimistic and exultant. Heller, for instance, wrote, "We have good reason to expect the U.S. economy to advance more steadily and, on average, more rapidly than either its long-run real growth rate of about 3 percent or its postwar rate of 3½ to 4 percent." And "The significance of the great expansion of the 1960s lies not in its striking statistics of employment, income, and growth but in its glowing promise of things to come."[12]

The high spirits were not confined to the economics profession. Successes of the New Economists gave the profession unprecedented popularity with the press, the business world, and the public. The acclaim was capped in 1968 by extending the Nobel Prize to include an annual award in the field of economics. As *Business Week* put it in 1966, the record of "remarkable growth—and remarkable stability—in the U.S. economy . . . has raised the prestige of economists—especially those who espouse the so-called new economics—to an all-time high."[13]

But by the late 1960s a new form of economic problem began to emerge. Keynesian policies seemed as helpless to cope with this new phenomenon as the free market prescriptions had been during the Great Depression. Economists had been aware that full employment could not be achieved without some upward pressure on prices, but it was generally thought that a tradeoff existed between employment and inflation. The Phillips Curve predicted that unemployment rates above 5 percent would correlate with price deflation, while price inflation would surpass 4 percent only when rates of unemployment went below 2 percent. And, in fact, between 1952 and 1967 the facts conformed closely to these expectations: Inflation stayed below 4 percent, and unemployment varied between 4 and 7 percent. But, as shown in Figure 2-2, a different picture emerged in the 1970s. Neither inflation nor unemployment has gone under 4 percent; and by 1974 inflation had hit 14.6 percent and official unemployment had soared to over 7 percent.

Lacking a coherent explanation, the New Economists generally blame a "confluence of random accidents." In the 1974 presidential address to the American Economics Association, Heller defended the New Economics: "It is asking a lot of economists to expect them to have foreseen that the oil cartel would quadruple oil prices, that the world would suffer widespread and successive crop failures, that the Peruvian anchovies would go into hiding, and that the Soviet Union would 'solve our surplus grain problem' overnight."[14] James Tobin, another Kennedy advisor and author of *The New Economics: One Decade Older,* notes an unexpected steepness to the Phillips Curve at less than 4 percent unemployment rates, but he provides no explanation. He offers a series of minor modifications in fiscal and monetary policies that he believes, once the dislocations caused by the Vietnam War are over, will ensure a rebound in status for the New Economics.[15]

Milton Friedman, as expected, places the blame on the government: "The plain fact is that inflation is made in Washington, in . . . the Federal Reserve System. . . . The government produces inflation, nobody but the government can produce inflation." Friedman asks, "Why does the Fed remain an engine of inflation? I confess that I am baffled."[16]

While the coexistence of inflation and unemployment creates a theoretical paradox for the mainstream economists, it creates a se-

Figure 2-2 Divergence of Actual Unemployment-Inflation Conditions from the Phillips Curve

Source: Position of Phillips Curve from Paul Samuelson, *Economics,* 8th ed. (New York: McGraw-Hill, 1970), p. 810. Actual data from *Economic Report of the President, 1975,* Tables C-24 and C-44.

vere policy dilemma for the government. Successful stabilization policies had been based upon two crucial ideas. The first one was that unemployment and inflation are opposites, occurring not simultaneously but in a tradeoff relation. Unemployment was said to be caused by insufficient demand and inflation by excess demand; controlling the first therefore called for expansionary government policies and controlling the second, for contractionary policies. But since inflation and unemployment have now occurred together, government action to relieve one condition would exacerbate the other automatically. For example, using easy money to reduce unemployment would increase inflation, and using tight fiscal policy to fight inflation would increase unemployment.

The second Keynesian assumption was that perpetually high rates of growth are possible. According to Okun's Law, there is a fixed relation between the rate of real growth and unemployment: Given the current United States rates of population increase and labor productivity gains, an annual rate of growth of 4 percent is required to maintain any given level of unemployment.[17] At 4 percent growth in production new jobs just match the new entrants into the labor force. Furthermore, changes in unemployment show a one-to-three relation to changes in the growth rate: Every 3 percent change in the growth rate will change the unemployment rate by only 1 percent. Okun gives no real theoretical explanation for his "law"; he only reports an observed correlation.

But, as demonstrated in Figure 2-3, the implications are obvious and gloomy. Merely to maintain the 1975 unemployment rate at 9 percent, the United States economy must grow 4 percent each year. To reduce unemployment to 5.5 percent, or roughly 5 million workers, the economy must grow at an annual rate of 6 percent for five years. However, the United States economy has never grown at such

Figure 2-3 Unemployment in 1980 Given Three Projected Growth Rates

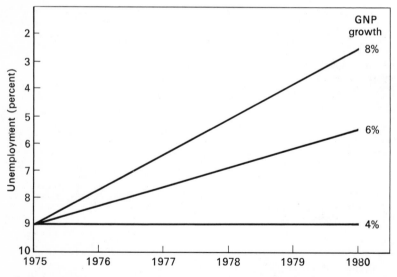

Source: Fortune (June 1975), p. 85. Reprinted by permission, *Fortune* Art Department/Vahé Kirishjian. All three lines are plotted according to Okun's Law

a rate, except during World War II and the 1962–1966 period, when inflation was not a threat. And to reduce unemployment to 2.5 percent (over 2 million without work by government count) the economy must grow at the real rate of 8 percent for at least five years. Clearly, if Okun's Law is true, the 1970s will be a decade of high unemployment. In fact, one study estimates that 36 million new jobs would be required to reduce unemployment to 5 percent by 1985; this is twice as many jobs as were created in the previous ten years.[18]

Both high unemployment and inflation then, have returned with a vengeance, and the technical solutions promised by the New Economics do not fit the new circumstances. The New Economics was an advance over the free market perspective in that it provided both an explanation of involuntary unemployment and policy measures for ending the Great Depression. Nevertheless, as a theory of crisis, the New Economics concentrates on the effects of *expenditures,* while a Marxian perspective emphasizes contradictions in the *production process.*

Let us look briefly at this alternative view. Increased production depends upon the expansion of the stock of capital. The source of capital accumulation is the investable surplus left over after all labor, material costs of production, interest, and taxes have been deducted from revenues.

In the earlier, highly competitive phase of capitalism the expansionary process was propelled by competition among capitalists, each investing all available surplus in pursuit of greater profits and fearing that failure to do so would lead to technological obsolescence and financial ruin. The instability of the system flowed from the gap between the capacity to consume and the expanded capacity to produce. Put another way, the pursuit of profits by individual capitalists created a cumulative effect of overexpansion of productive capacity relative to consumption capacity. Seen from the viewpoint of the owners, the workers played two incompatible roles: as producers their low wages would create a higner investable surplus and potential capital accumulation; as consumers their higher wages would create larger markets for capitalist products. To the extent that capitalists were successful in keeping wages down, their selling problem was intensified by a lack of demand; to the extent that workers were successful in driving wages up, the accumulation process was impeded by a lack of investable surplus.

The lack of an overall planning mechanism led periodically to imbalance between the capacity to produce and the capacity to consume. This had to be corrected by substantial adjustments in patterns of production and consumption. The market mechanism celebrated by the free market perspective might eventually correct the imbalance, but the adjustments might not be made for months or years. In the meantime, the economy would face a crisis, with production, profits, wages, and employment spiraling downward. This interpretation of economic crisis bears a superficial similarity to the Keynesian theory of crisis caused by underspending. But, in fact, there is an important distinction: The Keynesian theory traces the cause of crisis to the motives of the business community to invest or hoard and to the choices of consumers to consume or save, while the Marxian view reveals how the very competition among capitalists creates a cleavage between the system's capacity to produce and the consumers' capacity to purchase products. The dislocations, as conceived by the Keynesians, can be resolved by government pump priming to encourage consumer spending. But according to the Marxian theory, pump priming will treat historically specific symptoms while leaving the underlying tendencies toward instability intact.

In short, just as the Great Depression smashed the credibility of Say's Law, the stagflation of the early 1970s demolished the notion of fine tuning the capitalist economy to sustain full employment, high growth, price stability, and a strong dollar in world markets. History applies a stern test to economic doctrines. The New Economists underestimated or ignored changes in the structure of corporate capitalism within which monetary and fiscal instruments were applied. Some of these changes flowed from the very forms assumed by government economic policy. We turn now to an analysis that illuminates these structural changes.

Stagflation and Corporate-State Expansion

The nature of the expansionary process today has been altered by two recent structural changes in the political economy of corporate capitalism: (1) the transition from the competitive, small-scale firm of the mid-nineteenth century to the monopolistic, corporate giant of the mid-twentieth century, and (2) the emergence of the state as a dominant force in shaping economic expansion. These structural changes have had far-reaching effects on pricing behavior and cost conditions and, we will argue, have qualitatively changed the nature of economic crisis. If we are correct, important implications arise for the improvement of economic conditions, for the roots of the problem are in the system of production for private profit.

Monopolistic Pricing Power

The moderate price rises of the early 1960s were perceived by the New Economists as a necessary accompaniment to a booming economy. But the New Economists did not account for the fact that in the face of sluggish growth and slack demand prices rose by 50 percent in the 1967–1975 period. Every year of the 1970s has meant unemployment for at least 4 million workers by official count and excess productive capacity levels of greater than 20 percent (except briefly in 1973). The coexistence of rising prices and excess supply is impossible in a competitive market setting, for, by definition, excess supply signifies falling prices. To explain this pairing, we must start (but not end) by examining pricing behavior in the light of the shift from competitive to monopolistic markets.

In the 1870s the American economy was composed mainly of small, one-product, geographically bounded, owner-managed firms operating in competitive markets. And, as shown in Figure 2-4, with the exception of two war periods, prices throughout the 1800s moved downward. But between the years of 1897 and 1905 the first of three great merger movements transformed business firms and market structures. The impact on the shape of American industry is described in a major study of merger activities:

> *It transformed many industries, formerly characterized by many small and medium-sized firms, into those in which one or a few*

Figure 2-4 Consumer Price Index, 1800–1975 (1967 = 100)

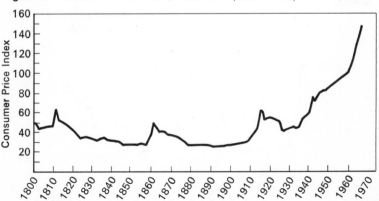

Source: Handbook of Labor Statistics, 1971 (U.S. Department of Labor, 1971), p. 253.

*very large enterprises occupied leading positions. It laid the
foundation for the industrial structure that has characterized
most of American industry in the twentieth century.*[19]

A second wave of merger activity from 1925 to 1930 firmly established most of the giant national corporations of today and the basic
contours of today's industrial market structure. By the end of that
period three or four firms had established a dominant position in
several areas, including automobile, oil, steel, and tires.[20] The new
businesses served a national market, sold several products, established a complex, administrative apparatus, and sold stocks to the
public.[21] Profit was, as always, the key to survival, but barriers to
entry, especially sheer size, greatly reduced the risk of being under-
sold. Market control over the behavior of these firms was thus reduced.[22]

As shown in Figure 2-5, the third great merger movement peaked
in the late 1960s. From 1965 to 1971, 10,835 total mergers were
recorded, compared to 2864 mergers in the seven-year turn-of-the-
century movement and 4682 during the six years 1925–1930.[23] Between 1948 and 1968 the 200 largest manufacturing corporations

Figure 2-5 Merger Activity in Manufacturing and Mining

Sources: William G. Shepherd, *Market Power and Economic Welfare* (New York:
Random House, 1970), p. 71. Broken line represents a use of data sources that
are not entirely comparable. Recent data are from Bureau of Economics, Federal
Trade Commission.

acquired 3684 firms worth about $50 billion. Whereas in 1909 the 100 largest industrial firms owned 17.7 percent of all manufacturing assets, by 1968 they owned 48.8 percent. The largest 272 firms, each with assets of over $250 million, made 69 percent of all manufacturing profits in the first quarter of 1968.[24] Summarizing the growth of the 500 largest industrial corporations over the 1954–1974 period, *Fortune* magazine noted the following:

> In general, the 500's share of the industrial economy has been rising over the years. Their share of total industrial sales rose from around half in 1954 to around two thirds last year. Their share of earnings, which fell last year, is nevertheless up from two thirds to three quarters over the two decades. And while the 500's share of industry has risen in this period, the manufacturing and mining shares of total GNP have also been rising a bit in real terms (to a little over one quarter). There is no doubt, then, that the 500 largest industrials are a substantially greater chunk of the U.S. economy than they were when Fortune *began compiling these lists* [in 1954].[25]

By 1974 four firms or less accounted for 50 percent or more of total sales in nearly two thirds of all manufacturing.[26]

In purely competitive markets the output of each firm is such a small fraction of the total output that no single firm can affect market prices. In monopolistic markets the sales of a single firm are large enough to affect market supply and price. Since, in this setting, the action of each firm affects the profitability of all firms in the industry, monopolistic firms develop group pricing strategies. Conscious of their interdependence, monopolistic firms behave more as price makers than as price takers. Although direct evidence is understandably sparse on the pricing strategies of corporations, it is quite clear that independent firms follow price markup strategies: Prices are set high enough to cover average industry costs plus a margin for profits. Any cost rises that are general to the industry, such as higher wages, energy, material, interest or tax payments, or higher unit costs caused by reduced production levels, will be passed on to consumers as higher prices.

It is also evident that prices rarely drop in monopolistic industries, even under conditions of slack demand; for all firms know that if one firm were to reduce prices a price war might develop in which all firms would lose. Instead, products are withheld from the market. When demand is slack, monopoly firms would rather withhold some products to maintain a high price.[27] Thus monopolistic firms characteristically maintain a margin of unused or excess productive capacity. The *planned* margin protects their market share if demand suddenly spurts up. The *unplanned* margin is generated by the vicissitudes of the business cycle.

If our reasoning is correct, we would expect to find very different pricing responses to declining demand in monopolistic and competitive industries. Several recent empirical studies have corroborated this claim. One economist, studying the behavior of sixteen pairs of products, one of each in an oligopolistic and the other in a competitive industry, found a notable difference in the price responses to slack demand. During the two recessions of the 1950s the price indices of every competitive industry fell, whereas in thirteen of sixteen of the concentrated industries the price index rose.[28] Another study found that in the September 1973 to September 1974 period of plummeting sales (excess capacity increased 25 percent, unemployment 23 percent) wholesale prices in "concentration dominated industries" *rose* 27 percent. In "competition dominated industries" the price rise was less than 5 percent.[29] Thus the increased concentration of American industry helps to explain the trend toward rising prices maintained since World War II, for during this era, initial periods of price inflation were not followed by periods of price deflation.

Notice the limited extent of our claim. The power of the monopolistic firm to administer prices does not give it sufficient power to set profit margins in all situations, nor is this new power alone the cause of economic instability. The capacity of monopolistic firms to raise prices in concert does not oblige consumers to purchase at the higher prices. Consumers may discontinue purchase of the product or, especially since the postwar reconstruction of the economies of Western Europe and Japan, purchase foreign products. Higher prices can reduce sales enough to reduce profits and thereby drive up unit costs.[30] As shown in Figure 2-6, recent history suggests a strong positive correlation between profits and variations in capacity utilization.[31]

Monopolistic pricing, then, has two effects: First, monopolistic firms introduce an upward bias in prices even during periods of slack demand. The upward pressure is accentuated by increased production costs, which, we argue later, have been rising because of the form assumed by corporate-state expansion in the post-World War II period.

Second, monopolistic price setting contributes to instability by hampering both market and government adjustments to changes in

Figure 2-6 Profits and Capacity Utilization

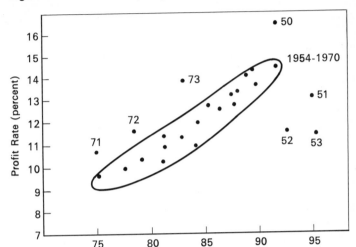

Capacity Utilization Rate (actual output ÷ productive capacity)

Source: Economic Report of the President, 1975, Tables C-37 and C-76.

the conditions of supply and demand. When demand is slack and prices do not adjust downward (as they would under competitive conditions), this inflexibility can in fact intensify the downturn. For example, if the response of business to a slackening in demand is to build up inventories and lay off workers (instead of reducing prices and thereby stimulating demand), then the downturn would be intensified by a reduction in spending power. Monopolistic price setting can also reduce the effectiveness of government deflationary policies. When the government reduces expenditures, imposes higher taxes, or increases interest rates, the monopolistic firm does not necessarily reduce prices. It might withhold products to keep prices up. Under these conditions the anti-inflation measures of the New Economics can be counterproductive: Measures such as higher taxes or higher interest rates, designed to curb demand, in fact generate higher costs and can encourage price increases.

The monopolistic firm creates a climate in which prices do not fall when demand slackens and in which a gap between sales and productive capacity is maintained. This, however, is only part of the story. The imperative of monopoly profitability also has important consequences for determining where investments are made, where labor is employed, and what goods are produced. As we will see, the incompatibility between social needs and private profit has deepened in recent years.

Rising Costs of Production

In the 1930s the productive capacity of capital overshot the capacity of consumers to buy and thus led to a depression. In response to the failure of unregulated capitalism to revive itself the state tried to stimulate and guide the expansionary process. State intervention succeeded in correcting the production/consumption imbalance, but the solution itself generated a new environment in which new barriers to economic expansion and capital accumulation eventually emerged.

Some features of the stagflation of the 1970s are characteristic of previous recessions: Corporations face profit squeezes and debt buildup; government is confronted with fiscal crises; workers face increased insecurity and unemployment; living standards deteriorate. Thus profits have followed a familiar cyclical pattern, dropping from 10 percent on invested capital in 1965–1966 to between 5 and 6 percent in 1970–1973.[32] The source of the profit squeeze, however, is not the old divergence between productive and consumption capacities.

Thirty years of state support for corporate giants has helped to foster an extremely irrational system of production. This system has squeezed profits by driving up costs in four ways:

1. The imperatives of corporate profitability have created new living expenses for workers, thereby increasing wage demands and labor costs to owners.
2. Government expenditures in response to accumulated dislocations created by the private sector have increased the tax payments of both labor and capital.
3. The unplanned production system has become increasingly dependent upon foreign resources (especially energy) that are in short and insecure supply, thereby increasing the cost of resources in production.
4. A greatly expanded corporate and government debt load built up by the prolonged post-World War II expansionary boom has magnified borrowing costs.

As these costs accumulate, the investable surplus (as a proportion of investment needs) declines, forcing a slowdown in the growth of productive capacity. The system of production for private profit, bolstered by state priming and subsidies, has once again, though in a distinctively new way, tied itself into knots. It has channeled enormous amounts of labor, capital, material, and resources into military and space programs, expansion of the highway transportation system, the energy delivery consortium, and the private health insurance empire. Today the economy is a prisoner of such past investment; little is left over after meeting the capital requirements of these political–economic empires.

To document and illustrate these general claims, we will examine several ways in which the state and monopolistic capital create new costs that increase burdens upon citizens and undermine the expansionary objectives of private owners and public officials. Military expenditures, the proliferation of irrational products, welfare state expenditures, and the alienated organization of work will each receive our attention. These features of advanced capitalism, translated into new costs of production and living, are also converted into higher prices by monopoly firms. But limits on the price setting power further reduce the investable surplus available to firms and increases their dependence on debt to finance further growth. This latest phase in the development of the system's tendency toward instability will be examined in a later section.

Costs of Militarism

The success of the New Economics in the post-World War II period rests heavily upon armament production. Government military expenditures provide markets for corporations and spur economic growth without placing government enterprises in competition with private companies (socialized production), flooding the market with consumer goods and thereby reducing prices, or reducing worker dependence on corporate employment (as would guaranteed annual income or public service employment). Furthermore, the military establishment protects the country abroad and helps to dampen opposition to corporate autonomy at home.

Out of the total federal purchases of $1.5 trillion between 1946 and 1971, $1.1 trillion was defense-related spending (including debt payments for previous wars, veteran benefits, space, and Atomic Energy Commission).[33] Without this spending (or equivalent spending in some other area that does not compete with corporate sales), unemployment rates in the postwar period would approximate those of the Great Depression. Thus in 1970 there were 2.9 million members of the armed forces, 1.2 million civilian employees in the Defense Department, and 3.0 million employees in defense industries.

This total, over 7 million, includes only those directly dependent on military spending. If one assumes a multiplier effect of 1, a conservative estimate, another 7 million are indirectly dependent on military spending.[34] If to these first two categories of military-dependent employees we add the 7.9 million unemployed in 1970, the total comes to 22.2 million workers, or about 26 percent of the labor force, a figure slightly higher than the highest level of unemployment during the Great Depression. Without extensive military expenditures, then, it is not clear that Keynesian policies would have dissolved the unemployment of the Great Depression or even maintained tolerable levels of employment in the 1960s.

But the stimulant side of militarism in the 1960s has given way to the depressant side of militarism in the 1970s. Whereas in the context of the 1960s the positive effects on growth and employment dominated public awareness, the fiscal crises and tax revolts of the 1970s have made its negative side painfully clear. Military production diverts resources from production for useful goods; in fact, consumers pay approximately 8 percent of their annual income in real goods forgone to finance the military budget. In other words, all American workers could have had more than an extra month of paid vacation annually if the same resources had gone to useful goods instead of to militarism.

The costs of the Southeast Asian war illustrate the point. Using the most conservative estimates, which put the ultimate cost of the war at $350 billion, we can say that the United States government could have paid off instead the mortgage on every home in America, with money left over. One study estimates that the $90 to $100 billion spent on the war during the 1960s was fourteen times more than support for all levels of education or several times what the United States has spent in its entire history for public higher education. Another economist estimated that after all expenses are covered, the same war will cost closer to $900 billion, which means that on the average "every American alive in 1969 will spend approximately one year of his life working to pay the cost of the Vietnam War."[35] Militarism is as effective as the drug that eliminated the symptom (lack of effective demand) but killed the patient (the public).

Regardless of the costs, military expenditures will not be easily reduced. Once investment moves into areas that are privately profitable, new political constituencies, dependent on these industries for profit and employment, emerge to protect and extend these corporate complexes. Government policy then has to work with and around the complexes it created itself as it tries to tune the economy in the new, more treacherous environment. Today government policymakers must continue to feed this dinosaur or be devoured by it.

Costs of Irrational Products

Under competitive capitalism the market forced individual firms into product designs and output decisions that drove prices down. In the process, costs to all capitalists were also driven down. For example, take the staple commodity wheat. Between 1859 and 1884 wheat production increased from 173 to 468 million bushels; the price of a bushel of wheat was $1.24 in 1871; by 1894 it sold for 49 cents.[36] By driving down the price of a crucial wage good, the individual firms' pursuit of profit benefited all firms by driving down costs: the costs of wages paid to workers.

Automobiles provide a similar example for a later period. When the Model T was introduced in 1908 it sold for $1000; by 1924 it cost $300.[37] However, in the monopolistic market the Big Three automakers compete more over annual style changes than they do over prices and quality. In 1969 they spent $1.5 billion on model changes, and according to the Bureau of Labor Statistics there was a $3 decrease in car performance.[38] As profitable as the operation is for the automobile industry, it is costly for employers as a class. Each worker must be paid more wages to pay for cars and highways.

Energy and health care, major items in the family budget, are also dominated by monopoly complexes. America's postwar patterns of energy use, although highly lucrative to the major oil companies, have driven many consumers and some firms to insolvency with the price rises of the 1970s.[39] Neglecting the needs of many, the health empire maximizes profits by specializing on high-cost, private, curative medicine to the exclusion of cheaper preventive health care. The National Cancer Institute, for example, estimates that 80 percent of cancers are environmentally caused.[40] Yet the health empire has done little to alert Americans to the connections between environmental pollution and health. Why? Part of the answer may be that it is more profitable to doctors, drug, hospital, insurance, and associated interests to concentrate on cures.

Product quality is yet another casualty of production for profit under monopolistic market conditions. Profits are maximized for the industry as long as no single firm steps out of line by producing a durable quality product at a reasonable price. For example, *The Economist* reported in 1969 that a company had developed a new light bulb, lasting twice as long as bulbs on the market. But it was withheld from the market.[41] The reason is clear enough. Production of quality-improving innovations would diminish the market by reducing the need for replacements.[42]

Production geared to social use rather than corporate profit would require basic changes in the nature of the firm and its public accountability. But the rest of us would benefit immensely. Annual auto model changes, which add between $500 and $1000 to the cost of a car without improving its quality, would end.[43] Consumers could divert funds now tied to the replacement of worn out products to more functional purchases. It would mean a vast reduction in ineffective beauty and diet aids, useless drugs, worthless auto repairs, and similar forms of irrational production.

But the escalation of consumer expenses is only partly explained by the production of irrational low-quality goods. The system of production for profit has also generated new consumer needs over the last thirty years that are translated into expanded consumer expenses. Growth based on private profitability rather than social usefulness has ravaged large portions of the natural environment. Needs formerly met by personal effort or simply through nature's abundance must increasingly be met by the economic system. Consumers look more and more to the economic system to "produce" a habitat free from industrial noise and waste, health services to compensate for the unhealthy urban environment, education to compete in modern labor markets, and the clean air, pure water, healthy sunshine, and open space that were free goods in an earlier era. Much consumption is involuntary. Those who consume gases, chemicals, dust, and criminal assaults at work and play must then compensate, however imperfectly, through increased expenditures for insurance, health, cleaning, and police protection. Each new consumer or public need in areas previously met by nature or by a harmonious community atmosphere generates increased expenses without improving the real welfare of the recipients. It follows, then, that workers' wage demands are not tied simply to productivity advances and profit margins at their places of employment; higher wages can be necessary to compensate for a deteriorating natural and social environment.

In summary, products have two sides: a *use* value to the society and a *profit* value to the seller. The two values can diverge: Public parks have a high use value and a low profit value; adulterated meats have a low use value and a high profit value. We also noted a third side to each product: the profit value to *all firms*, which has itself diverged from the profit value for *one firm*. That is, any single company accounts for the profitability of a particular product to that firm alone; it does not account for either the product's use value to society or the profitability to all firms taken together. We contend that monopoly market conditions have widened the gap between use values and profit values. Corporate owners, of course, do not see the roots of the problem. What they see is a growing wage and tax bill, squeezing profits. What they do in response is to raise prices. They think the source of the problem is the greediness of labor and the inefficiency of government. But they fail to understand that their own immediate desire for profits feeds the very wage, tax, and cost pressures they must later respond to. And unfortunately for monopolistic capital, the market adjustment mechanism that once drove down the price of wages by generating ever cheaper consumer products no longer operates effectively. It was a victim of the transition to corporate capitalism.

If we are on the right track, three implications follow. First, the intensification of worker demands for higher wages is less a greedy drive for affluence than a response to the structurally constrained context in which people must meet their needs for food, shelter, clothing, recreation, and education.

Second, profits are being squeezed, but the squeeze is not induced by falling prices in response to rising supply as predicted by the free market perspective, but by rising costs emanating from the irrationality of capitalist production.

A third implication is crucial for state policy: The split between production for profit and social needs that prevails in the 1970s is less responsive to government stabilization measures than the imbalance between production and consumption of the 1930s. The source of capital accumulation (profits from existing investments) is separated from the uses required for socially productive investment (products that satisfy social needs). In other words, although the state can expand profits by stabilization policies, there is no assurance that the profits generated by stimulating the wasteful industrial complexes of the past will be transferred to the new socially productive areas. For example, the state could increase profits in the automobile industry by stimulating demand; but if the profits were then transferred to investments in mass transit, it is likely that the capital used to produce cars would substantially depreciate. Hence, left to the market, it is unlikely that increased profits will solve the accumulation problems of the 1970s. The corporate system of production for profits must be displaced by a publicly controlled system of production for use.

Welfare State Expenses

At the same time that the consumer as an individual (or as a breadwinner for a nuclear family) has developed new needs, collective expenses have also multiplied. Our transportation system, built around energy wasting and polluting vehicles such as the car, the plane, and the truck, generates an expensive public infrastructure of highways, airports, traffic control systems, expanded police forces, and subsidies to energy producers. The technical requirements of work in an automated society become public costs of financing higher education. The relatively high levels of unemployment and underemployment sustained by the private productive system require an extensive public welfare system. The breakdown of extended kinship ties, fostered to some degree by the individual mobility necessary to gain employment and advancement in America, expands the role of the state in meeting the needs of the elderly, the infirm, the handicapped, the retarded. The mechanization of agriculture, for example, helped to expand the welfare roles in the cities. It is not that the state should refuse to meet these costs, once the need has been created. But many of the needs themselves are rooted more in the priorities of corporate capitalism than in the functional requirements of industrial society per se.

Each dislocation flowing from private corporate practices eventually becomes a public problem, a problem for the state to resolve through the taxation of citizens. Unable to shape corporate priorities, people nonetheless feel the social effects, either as victims of unemployment or as taxpayers paying a growing share of their incomes to meet military, highway, education, and welfare expenditures. Caught in the squeeze between proliferating private expenses and expanding tax obligations, citizens are likely to support deficit spending to finance government expenditures, even when the rules of capitalist economics would counsel against it. They are less the source of the resulting inflationary pressures than the conveyers of these pressures to the government.

Alienation and Wage Costs

In the United States the rate of increase in labor productivity has slowed from earlier levels and lagged behind those of Western Europe and Japan.[44] If wage increases surpass productivity gains, either a reduction in profits or a rise in consumer prices will follow. In 1974, while output per work-hour (labor productivity) in the private sector was only 12 percent higher than in 1967, labor compensation was 64 percent higher, producing a 47 percent rise in unit labor costs for the period.[45] Since the monopoly corporation is able to pass these new costs along to consumers in the form of higher prices, and since the government validates these price increases through inflationary policies, this gap between productivity gains and labor costs clearly contributed to inflation. John Kenneth Galbraith and several other economists at opposite positions within mainstream economics agree that much of recent inflation has been cost-push inflation, the push coming to some large degree from worker wage demands. But why have worker demands been so great during this period? And why has productivity grown so slowly? A large part of the answer to the first question has already been given. And we think one additional factor helps to answer both questions together, though the extent of its influence is extremely difficult to gauge.

A spate of recent studies of white- and blue-collar "blues," studies that we will examine in some detail in Chapter 5, indicate that workers are increasingly dissatisfied with the dangerous, unhealthy, uninteresting, authoritarian, repetitive conditions of work to which they are subjected. This disaffection, not easily converted into effective pressure for work reform in our system of political economy, may be translated into other areas where the worker can apply some leverage. It is no doubt translated, first, into higher rates of absenteeism and turnover, wildcat strikes, product sabotage, declining quality controls, and malingering on the job. Second, it intensifies demands for higher wages, the worker trying to make up during leisure time for the drudgery of work time. These two pressures together contribute to lower productivity and higher wages, enhancing inflationary tendencies. Corporate elites would rather acquiesce in these inflationary pressures—which they can then blame on government—than in the need for work reform itself. For to accept meaningful reform in the structure of work would be to weaken owner control over workers and the work process, creating leverage for more basic incursions into corporate prerogatives at a later date. Once again, the priorities of corporate capitalism generate grievances for workers (and consumers and citizens) while channeling their demands into public areas that protect corporate dominance, deepen inflationary pressures, and eventually weaken public support for liberal government policies.

The Debt Economy

In the postwar period the tendency for productive capacity to outrun markets was countered by growing government military and welfare expenditures and by a host of policies that intensified consumer demand. The spending was financed in part, as it always is during economic expansions, by debt creation.

Debt had been driven to a low level by the long downturn of the 1930s, and the financial markets were once more capable of providing the liquidity for an economic expansion. But by the late 1960s over twenty years of debt expansion had, as always, overburdened the financial markets. An old contradiction was reasserting itself: Capitalism needs healthy financial markets to grow, yet capitalist growth undermines healthy financial markets.

In the past the down phase of the business cycle served to restore strained financial markets by forcing bankruptcy on the overcommitted and poorly managed and reorganization and consolidation on the survivors. But in the climate of the 1960s the government could not afford the traditional remedy, because it would threaten the survival of the largest corporations in America. As a result the old tendencies toward instability have changed in form: The new cycle is marked by upturns that tend toward double-digit inflation and downturns that threaten to bankrupt a substantial core of the economy. Since the government cannot allow giant corporations to go under, the policies it must adopt to protect them contribute to the next phase of the cycle. As we have argued, the Keynesian resolution of the instability of the 1930s created new problems in the 1970s, which force the government to intervene increasingly to keep the economy afloat while they undermine its ability to promote full employment and price stability.

As shown in Figure 2-7, consumer debt as a percentage of disposable personal income was leveling off by 1965. But, as illustrated in Figure 2-8, 1965 also marked a dramatic expansion in the ratio of corporate debt to gross corporate output. Corporate investment funds came increasingly from borrowed funds rather than internally generated earnings.[46] The borrowing was needed because of a steady fall in profit rates beginning in 1966, which pressed corporations into debt to bridge the gap between desired capital spending and retained profits.[47] As shown in Figure 2-9, if profits had maintained the rise of the first half of the decade, the need for corporate borrowing would have been much less. The year 1965 also marks the beginning of the Southeast Asian war buildup, which because of pressures from the antiwar movement the government financed through deficit spending rather than taxes.[48]

Such massive levels of deficit finance led *Business Week*, traditionally an optimistic supporter of corporate policies, to express grave concern that the Debt Economy, as it labeled the phenomenon, was getting out of hand. Its commentary held a tone of urgency:

Figure 2-7 Consumer Debt as a Percentage of Disposable Personal Income

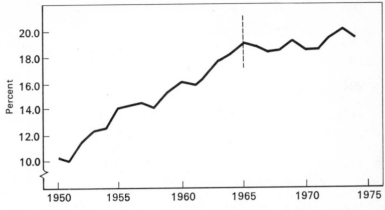

Source: Economic Report of the President, 1975, Tables C-18 and C-59.

Figure 2-8 Corporate Debt as a Percentage of Nonfinancial Corporate Product

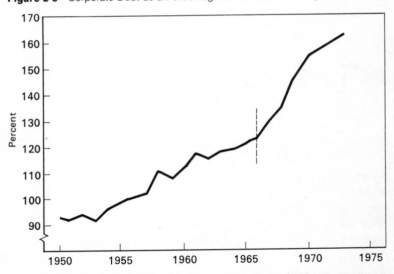

Source: Economic Report of the President, 1975, Tables C-11 and C-63.

"The Fed and the White House, petrified by both inflation and recession, seem unable to avoid swinging first this way and then that way; the dangers are greater than in the 1930s. . . . Never had the Debt

Figure 2-9 The Growing Capital Gap

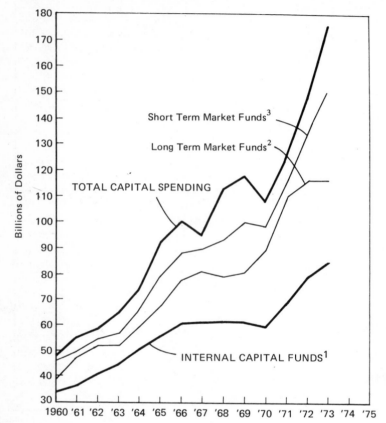

[1] Undistributed profits (after inventory adjustment) and capital consumption allowances.

[2] Stocks, bonds, mortgages.

[3] Bank loans, commercial paper, government loans, etc.

Source: Economic Report of the President, 1975, Table C-78.

Economy seemed so vulnerable."[49] Its concern was well founded. The huge debt was undermining the solvency of America's corporate giants. As *Newsweek* noted, some were hit especially hard: "The past few years have been littered with the case histories of firms like Penn Central, Lockheed, and Chrysler that have skated close to the financial precipice—and in some cases have gone over—because of heavy debt burdens."[50]

The proper relation between levels of debt and levels of production is a matter of some controversy, but it is clear that debt expansion cannot continue forever. By 1973 the debt of $2.5 trillion was eight times the nation's money supply, double the figure of twenty years before; and corporate debt, eight times greater than profits in 1953, and fifteen times greater in 1973.[51] The New York Stock Exchange estimates that $2.65 trillion will be needed for new plant, equipment, and inventory between 1975 and 1985. If these additions are financed as in the period from 1969 to 1973, corporate equity would increase by $500 billion, while corporate debt would grow by $750 billion. As *Business Week* has said: "Since the resulting interest burden would certainly bring about—well before 1985—the bankruptcy of most United States corporations, it is something less than desirable."[52]

Debt validation, that is, the ability to pay off debt, is determined by the spread between prices and costs to the corporation. Higher interest charges on a larger debt increase costs. Higher costs are forwarded to consumers in higher prices, which in turn elicit new rounds of higher interest rates. In this way interest, costs, and prices tend to chase each other upward until the inflationary spiral is broken and corporate debt is reduced. Therefore, corporate debt (and the health of financial markets) and prices (and the condition of product markets) are intertwined. The failure of the New Economists to consider the link between prices and debt led them to overestimate the stability of the system and the efficacy of fiscal and monetary policies. Rather than eliminating the fluctuations of the business cycle, as promised, the corporate-state interactions of the postwar period have actually created a new cycle of inflationary growth followed by liquidity squeezes.

As economic growth slackened between 1969 and 1971, capacity utilization dropped from 87.7 percent in 1968 to 75 percent in 1971, and profit rates fell from 12.1 percent to 9.7 percent.[53] Since the government was at that time financing the Southeast Asian war out of borrowed money (rather than taxes), the combined corporate-government demand for loans drove the interest rate to corporate borrowers to its highest level of the century. Corporations found themselves caught in a squeeze between declining profits and higher financing costs. The higher debt that had been profitable in good times turned into a substantial burden in bad times. By 1969–1970 a liquidity crisis (shortage of cash plus highly negotiable assets to debt) found many firms hard pressed to cover their debt costs. In the words of Tilford Gaines, vice president and economist of the Manufacturers Hanover Trust Company and former official of the Federal Reserve Bank of New York: "Short-term liabilities of business have skyrocketed in recent years while quick cash assets have been steady to declining," and in a disturbingly large number of companies across a band of industries, "survival questions have arisen." Months later Arthur Burns, chairman of the Federal Reserve Board, stated: "In permitting such a drastic decline in liquidity, many of our corporations openly courted trouble."[54] Reviewing the period, the report of the Joint Economic Committee on the *Economic Report of the President, 1972* notes, "The liquidity bind . . . in 1970 brought many to the edge of bankruptcy."

The implications for monetary policy were far-reaching. Faced with the threatened bankruptcy of a number of firms that were considerably bigger and more important to the economy than they had been at any time in history, the Fed either had to increase their liquidity by expanding the availability of credit or witness the probable failure of a number of giant corporations. As *Business Week* put it: "The huge U.S. corporations have become such important centers of jobs and incomes that it [the government] dare not let one of them shut down or go out of business. It is compelled, therefore to shape national policy in terms of protecting the great corporations instead of letting the economy make deflationary adjustments."[55]

The following quote from Arthur Burns describes the Fed's reactions to the major bankruptcy that did occur, the Penn Central:

> *By Monday, June 22 (1970)—the first business day following announcement of the bankruptcy petition—the Federal Reserve had already taken the virtually unprecedented step of advising the larger banks across the country that the discount window would be available to help the banks meet unusual borrowing requirements of firms that could not roll over the maturing commercial paper. . . . As a result of these prompt actions, a sigh of relief passed through the financial and business communities. . . . The financial community was assured that the Federal Reserve understood the seriousness of the situation and that it would stand ready to use its intellectual and financial resources, as well as its instruments of monetary policy, to assist the financial markets through any period of stress.*[56]

By the second half of 1970 the money supply (including savings deposits) was increasing at an annual rate of 10 percent, and it approached an annual rate of 20 percent in the first quarter of 1971. The increase in money bailed out many corporations by increasing the availability of credit and by forcing a real decline in the value of outstanding debt. Obviously, however, monetary policy was not being used to achieve the stated goals of the New Economists. The more fundamental concern of government was given primacy: to maintain the viability of giant corporations caught in a liquidity squeeze and to finance the Southeast Asian war.

But bailing corporations out of a liquidity squeeze by pumping up the money supply had a severe side effect: It created the conditions for a new round of inflationary expansion. And in the ensuing boom, corporate price increases, validated by the supply of new money, jumped upward to double-digit rates. Government policy was rapidly reversed. Anti-inflationary, or contractionary, policies (euphemism for sharply increasing the rate of unemployment to reduce demand) were enacted to guide the economy downward. Not only did the liquidity problems quickly reappear, this time they were worse. The precarious financial situation had by now spread to the banking system. As profits dropped and the stock market declined, corporations extended their borrowings from the banking system. The banks met the demands, but in the process the liquidity position of the large commercial banks fell sharply; liquid assets divided by deposits, which had been 54.0 percent in 1950, dropped from 22.3 percent in 1965 to 13.6 percent in 1974.[57] In an unsuccessful effort to save the fourteenth largest bank, Franklin National, the Fed pumped over $1 billion into it.[58] Once again government monetary authorities geared their policies to ensure the financial viability of big business, in this case a large bank.

In the past the business cycle had forced companies to keep a better balance between their debts and their liquid assets. But that balance disappeared in the new setting. As the editors of the *Monthly Review* have shown, "a bloated financial superstructure" is a direct consequence of government "eliminating or greatly mitigating the downturns."[59] Government officials are forced into inflationary policies in order to relieve the liquidity squeeze created by the very success of the earlier patterns of economic growth. Since a few corporations have now become so important to the total profit and employment structure of the economy, the government cannot afford, politically or economically, to let them collapse.

Clearly, the emergence of the debt economy has made the economic system prone to inflation; furthermore it has paralyzed the major employment-creating weapon of the New Economics during downturns—deficit spending. Simon, Secretary of the Treasury, put it correctly: "There is no way to escape the basic dilemma presented by large government deficits. On the one hand, if the deficits cause a significant increase in the money supply, we have further inflation. On the other hand, if deficits are not permitted to increase the money supply, we must be prepared to endure tight credit and high interest rates."[60] That is, if the government today attempts to reduce unemployment by deficit spending, one of two consequences will follow. First, it might sell billions of dollars in bonds, greatly diminishing the loanable funds available to private borrowers and crowding out corporations in need of loans. Corporations will be caught in a liquidity squeeze, threatening the survival of many and reducing employment. Secondly, the government can finance the sale of bonds by printing new money, but the resulting inflation will create severe dislocations.[61] Therefore Keynesian policies of spurring employment through deficit spending today set into motion forces that will eventually reduce employment. Before the government can meet its responsibilities as defined in the Full Employment Act of 1946, it must wait for the financial markets to return to a healthy condition, a process that financial authorities predict will take up the decade of the 1970s. This is but one of the many binds facing government policies in the contemporary system of corporate capitalism.

The Closing Cycle

Underlying the shift from an unemployment-inflation cycle to periodic eruptions of stagflation is the fundamental tendency toward instability in corporate capitalism. This tendency, though, is not endemic to industrial society as such. A system organized around production for use rather than production for profit would not necessarily oscillate in these ways. It could reduce the *costs of production* and the *social costs flowing from the productive system* by creating a public transportation system that reduces energy use and pollution emissions. It could develop more efficient forms of energy production, improve the ratio of collective goods to private consumer goods, produce durable housing, provide jobs for all citizens willing to work, and control inflation. Addressing the structural sources of instability, it could distribute the burdens and benefits of industrial society more evenly across the population and through time.

The historical tendency toward instability in corporate capitalism is experienced by common people as a recurrent struggle for security. Just as this tendency finds various expressions—first as inflation then as unemployment; once as liquidity squeeze, now as stagflation—the struggle for security itself assumes various modes among different sectors of the population. The young, especially blacks and working-class whites, find themselves frozen out of a production system that does not need their services. Old people, public sector workers, and unorganized workers in the market sector struggle to make ends meet as inflation outruns income gains. Mothers in working-class families seek second jobs at marginal pay, stretching the family income to meet growing food, clothing, utility, and tax bills. Middle-aged white-collar workers, straining to meet skyrocketing expenses in higher education so that their children will have a chance for good jobs, find themselves in conflict with young people, who threaten the job security so recently and precariously won.

While social tensions simmer, the business cycle, modestly responsive to fiscal and monetary fine tuning during the early 1960s, has acquired a new immunity to the old inoculations. And for good reason. Unattuned to the inner connections among corporate concentration, economic inequality, the irrationality of corporate product priorities and debt accumulation, the deadening structure of work, the bloated growth of the warfare-welfare state, the New Economists are thereby unprepared as the consequences of these structural tendencies penetrate into the unemployment-inflation cycle itself. They are the last to learn the painful lesson: Fine tuning will not fix a machine in need of an overhaul.[62]

NOTES

1. All official unemployment data are from *Economic Report of the President* (Washington: Government Printing Office, 1975). Data on the number and lengths of recessions are from Maurice Flamant and Jeanne Singer-Kerel, *Modern Economic Crises and Recessions* (New York: Harper and Row, 1970).

2. Bertram Gross and Stanley Moss estimate that real unemployment for 1971 was 24.6 percent of the labor force. They include 5 million housewives (1 of 7) and 4 million people between the ages of 55 and 64 (1 of 2) who have been "pushed out" of the labor force. See "Real Unemployment Is Much Higher Than They Say," in *Public Service Employment: An Analysis of Its History, Problems and Prospects*, ed. Alan Gartner et al. (New York: Praeger, 1973), pp. 30–36.

3. Harry Magdoff and Paul Sweezy, "Capitalism and Unemployment," *Monthly Review* (June 1975), pp. 1–14. Magdoff and Sweezy add:

"And it should be stressed that the 13.6 percent is still an understatement, due to the conservative nature of assumptions we made."

4. The estimate of three times is based on data in *Manpower Report of the President* (Washington: Government Printing Office, 1975), pp. 274–276, cited in Magdoff and Sweezy.

5. Douglas F. Dowd, *The Twisted Dream: Capitalist Development in the United States Since 1776* (Cambridge, Mass.: Winthrop, 1974), p. 161.

6. All the following extracts are from *Hard Times: An Oral History of the Great Depression*, by Studs Terkel. Copyright © 1970 by Studs Terkel. Reprinted by permission of Pantheon Books, a division of Random House, Inc., and Penguin Books, Ltd.

7. The effects of a minimum wage imposed by either a labor union or the government are shown in the accompanying diagram. Assume an equilibrium wage and employment situation at W_e and E_e and a minimum wage set (either by a labor union or government) at W_i (wage with intervention). Below W_i the new supply of labor will no longer be determined by the free choice of labor (the original labor supply curve) but will instead run along the minimum wage line until it reaches the original labor supply curve at the minimum wage level. The wage with intervention will be higher but at the expense of a loss of jobs for $E_e - E_i$ workers. In fact, at the prevailing wage, W_i, those willing to work but unable to find a job are indicated by the gap between the demand and original supply of labor at the minimum wage rate, W_i.

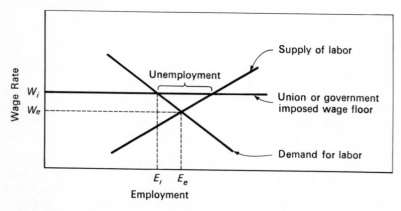

8. *The General Theory of Employment, Interest, and Money* (New York: Harcourt, Brace, 1936).

9. Ibid., p. 348.

10. Ibid., p. 348 for the Keynes quote. The dog analogy is by James E. Meade in *Essays on John Maynard Keynes*, ed. Milo Keynes (New

York: Cambridge University Press, 1975), cited in a review of same by Robert Lekachman in *Challenge* (September–October 1975), p. 63.

Put differently, the free market perspective, based on free choice and price adjustments, stresses a line of causation that begins with personal savings (individual choice to consume in the future rather than the present). For instance, a rise in savings will lead to an equal increase in investment via an interest rate adjustment. The resultant increase in capital will increase the levels of worker productivity and income. The Keynesian perspective, focusing on effective demand and employment adjustments, reverses the line of causation. Investment is the primary force. An expansion in investment operates via a multiplied expansion in employment to expand the level of income until sufficient savings are generated to match the higher level of investment. Thus, whereas in the free market perspective savings create investment and a lack of savings signifies a higher interest rate and more current consumption, in the Keynesian perspective investment creates savings and a lack of investment leads to unemployment and less consumption.

11. The successful tax cut of 1964, the major achievement of the New Economists, is amply described by two chairmen of the Council of Economic Advisors in the 1960s: Arthur M. Okun, *The Political Economy of Prosperity* (New York: Norton, 1970), and Walter W. Heller, *New Dimensions of Political Economy* (New York: Norton, 1967). The data in the text are from Heller, p. 114.

12. Heller, pp. 105 and 58. He goes on to predict a growth rate in GNP of between 4 and 4½ percent for the decade of the 1970s.

13. *Business Week*, February 5, 1966, p. 125. Cited in Heller, p. 3.

14. "What's Right with Economics," *American Economic Review* (March 1975), p. 8.

15. (Princeton, N.J.: Princeton University Press, 1974). Tobin, past president of the American Economics Association and member of the Council of Economic Advisors, remains optimistic about employment and growth: "Active monetary and fiscal policies, dedicated to economic ends and liberated from extraneous taboos, can keep the economy growing within a narrow band of full employment. Not again, I trust, will this hope, along with so many other national aspirations, be betrayed by a Vietnam." But Tobin ducks the inflation issue: "I have certainly not done justice to the subject of inflation in this book. As a consolation, I can only offer my opinion that inflation is greatly exaggerated as a social evil."

16. Milton Friedman, "The Inflationary Fed," *Newsweek*, August 27, 1973, p. 27, and *Congressional Record—Senate*, December 22, 1969, S 17529. Friedman notes a correlation between rising prices and growth in the money supply but fails to prove which comes first or to provide a convincing mechanism by which money supply increase

gets converted into higher prices as opposed to expanded output. For a critique of the monetarists, including Friedman, see Tobin, *The New Economics: One Decade Older.*

17. For a discussion of Okun's Law, see "The Slow Road Back to Full Employment," *Fortune* (June 1975), p. 84.

18. Magdoff and Sweezy, pp. 12–14. The 36 million comprises 8.2 million needed to reduce the current unemployment to 5 percent from 13.6 percent, 15.0 million required to accommodate population increase, and 12.8 million to compensate for productivity gains.

19. Ralph L. Nelson, *Merger Movements in American Industry, 1895–1956* (Princeton, N.J.: Princeton University Press, 1959). Cited in William N. Leonard, *Business Size, Market Power and Public Policy* (New York: Crowell, 1969).

20. For details about business concentration during this period, see G. Warren Nutter, *The Extent of Enterprise Monopoly in the United States* (Chicago: University of Chicago Press, 1951).

21. The sale of stocks does not mean that ownership is widely diversified. Various estimates conclude that 1–2 percent of the population own about three fourths of all corporate stocks and bonds, although the figures are complicated by the emergence of huge bank and insurance trust funds. See Robert J. Lampman, *The Share of Top Wealth-Holders in National Wealth, 1922–1956* (Princeton, N.J.: Princeton University Press, 1962); J. Smith and S. Franklin, "Concentration of Personal Wealth, 1922–69," *American Economic Review* (May 1974), p. 166; and chapter 3 of this text, "Inequality, the American Way."

22. For an analysis of barriers to entry and other industrial organization topics, see William G. Shepherd, *Market Power and Economic Welfare* (New York: Random House, 1970). In an examination of concentration and pricing power, Willard F. Mueller documents examples of huge price reductions following the breakup of price conspiracies: *A Primer in Monopoly and Competition* (New York: Random House, 1970), especially ch. 6. A *Business Week* article, "Price-Fixing: Crackdown Under Way," June 2, 1975, suggests that price fixing is widespread and that it pays.

23. Data on mergers are from Mueller.

24. Datum for 1909 is from Mueller, p. 69, and for 1968 from *Studies by the Staff of the Cabinet Committee on Price Stability* (Washington: Government Printing Office, 1969).

25. Linda Grant Martin, "The 500: A Report on Two Decades," *Fortune* (May 1975), p. 241.

26. Shepherd, Table 7.1, p. 106.

27. Ibid., p. 185.

28. John M. Blair, "Administered Prices—A Phenomenon in Search of a Theory," *American Economic Review* (May 1958), pp. 431–450.

29. Gardner Means, cited in *Consumer Reports* (June 1975), p. 380.

30. In a number of industries prices do not respond to shifts in demand as predicted by conventional economic theory of the firm. Prices are instead determined by markups over wage and material costs, the amount of the markup and profit being a function of the degree of monopoly that the firm exercises. For example, the prices of autos, steel, aluminum, appliances, and electrical equipment all rose during recessions of the 1950s and 1970s as the enterprises pursued a target rate of return over costs. For a theoretical treatment of pricing behavior under monopoly, see Paulo Sylos-Labini, *Oligopoly and Technical Progress* (Cambridge, Mass.: Harvard University Press, 1962), and Joan Robinson and John Eatwell, *An Introduction to Modern Economics* (New York: McGraw-Hill, 1973). For examples of industries that seek target rates of return as opposed to maximum short-term profits, see Leonard, *Business Size, Market Power and Public Policy*. Leonard estimates that "perhaps . . . one third of the rise of all consumer prices in the 1950s resulted from price policies of the steel oligopoly." In the 1970s examples of prices rising in the face of declining demand abound. Aluminum sales, for example, dropped by 7 percent in 1974 over 1973, yet profits stayed up as prices rose nearly 33 percent. Furthermore, prices have stayed up in the first quarter of 1975 even though sales dropped 40 percent! Robert Lindsey, "Aluminum Keeps the Price Up," *New York Times*, June 8, 1975, p. 1.

    The limits of the connection between the ability to set prices and the ability to set profit margins need more attention. The terms of relation between the corporate sector and the market sector of the economy may be pertinent here, as well as the relations between the state sector and the corporate sector. For example, price increases in the corporate sector may put a squeeze on market firms, thereby placing general economic expansion in peril. And government manipulation of the money supply might aim at expansion sufficient to keep large corporations afloat during a period of liquidity squeeze but insufficient to validate huge price increases. These and other possible connections need to be investigated more thoroughly.

31. For further analysis of the cyclical relations between profits and capacity utilization, see Paul A. Baran and Paul M. Sweezy, *Monopoly Capital* (New York: Monthly Review Press, 1966), ch. 4.

32. For these and other statistics on profits, see William D. Nordhaus, "The Falling Share of Profits," *Brookings Papers on Economic Activity*, no. 1 (1974), pp. 169–217.

33. Dowd, p. 105, and James L. Clayton, *The Economic Impact of the Cold War* (New York: Harcourt, Brace and World, 1970), pp. 51–54. Purchases do not include benefit payments to individuals or grants to state and local governments, since such spending does not directly use up resources by government agencies.

34. Data and multiplier estimate from Magdoff and Sweezy, pp. 1–14.

35. From studies cited by David Nyhan, "Indochina Cost Still Rising," *Boston Globe*, March 30, 1975, p. B-1. For perhaps the most detailed investigation, see Clayton. His figure of $352 billion for total cost of the Indochina war was adopted by the United States government's *Statistical Abstract*.

36. Dowd, p. 156. Wheat was not an isolated example. The wholesale price index for all commodities fell from 135 in 1872 to 69 in 1896.

37. Paul M. Sweezy, "Cars and Cities," *Monthly Review* (April 1973), p. 6.

38. Bradford C. Snell, "Annual Style Changes in the Automobile Industry as an Unfair Method of Competition," *Yale Law Journal* (December 1971), pp. 567–613.

39. Big Oil, which also controls major portions of alternative sources of energy such as gas, coal, atomic, and electrical energy, appears to have systematically restricted supply to expand profits. See *Wall Street Journal*, August 22, 1972 and March 27, 1974. And as Linda Charlton reports in the *New York Times*, they were highly successful: "Decades of Inaction Brought Energy Gap," February 10, 1974, p. 42.

40. See Barbara and John Ehrenreich, *The American Health Empire: Power, Profits and Politics* (New York: Vintage, 1971), and Joe Klein, "Interview with Ralph Nader," *Rolling Stone*, November 20, 1975, p. 57.

41. January 25, 1969, p. 64.

42. For more on the relation between quality deterioration and inflation, see Michael H. Best, "Notes on Inflation," *Review of Radical Political Economy* (August 1972), pp. 105–109.

43. Franklin M. Fisher, Zvi Grilliches, and Carl Kaysen estimated that annual model change costs came to about $700 for the 1956–1960 period: "The Costs of Automobile Model Changes Since 1949," *Journal of Political Economy* (October 1962), cited in Baran and Sweezy.

44. Gains in United States output per work-hour have lagged well behind its ten major competitors in world markets for recent years. In the 1965–1970 period the figures were as follows: U.S. 2.1, Belgium 6.8, Canada 3.5, France 6.6, Germany 5.3, Italy 5.1, Japan 14.2, Netherlands 8.5, Sweden 7.9, Switzerland 6.2, and U.K. 3.6. From Arthur Neef, "Unit Labor Costs in Eleven Countries," *Monthly Labor Review* (August 1971), p. 5.

45. Data from Economic Report of the President, 1975. For an alternative radical analysis of these data see Raford Boddy and James Crotty, "Class Conflict and Macro-Policy: The Political Business Cycle," *The Review of Radical Political Economics* (Spring 1975). Their model is based on changing shares of income and the business cycle. Economic expansion drives down the rate of unemployment, which pushes wages upward. The state then imposes a recession on the economy to reestablish capital's share of national income. The recession increases unemployment, which diminishes wage pressures and reestablishes the conditions necessary for profitable expansion.

46. Internal sources of corporate investment (undistributed profits plus depreciation allowances) dropped from 90 percent of total nonresidential investment in 1965 to 70 percent in 1970. From *Economic Report of the President, 1975*, Tables C-13 and C-74.

47. In a detailed study of postwar corporate profits, William D. Nordhaus estimates that before-tax returns steadily dropped from 16.3 percent of nonfinancial capital in 1965 to 9.1 percent in 1970; since then they have remained between 9 and 11 percent. He also estimates that corporate profits as a share of GNP fell from 11.0 percent in 1966 to a post-World War II low of 7.1 percent in 1970. See "The Falling Share of Profits."

48. For details on the mechanism of government debt finance as used to finance the Southeast Asian war, see Best.

49. "The Debt Economy," *Business Week,* October 12, 1974, p. 45.

50. "Will the Money Be There?" May 26, 1975, p. 64.

51. "The Debt Economy," p. 45.

52. Ibid., pp. 121–123.

53. Based on data from *Economic Report of the President, 1975.*

54. Gaines quote from *New York Times,* May 3, 1970; Burns quote from *New York Times,* December 8, 1970.

55. *Business Week,* January 27, 1975, p. 123.

56. *New York Times,* December 8, 1970.

57. Harry Magdoff and Paul M. Sweezy, "Banks Skating on Thin Ice," *Monthly Review* (February 1975), p. 12.

58. "Are the Banks Overextended?" *Business Week,* September 21, 1974, p. 54. See also Hyman Minsky, "Financial Resources in a Fragile Financial Environment," *Challenge* (July-August 1975), for an analysis of why banks have become increasingly fragile and for connections between debt and prices that are similar to our analysis.

59. Paul M. Sweezy and Harry Magdoff, "The Long-Run Decline in Liquidity," *Monthly Review* (September 1970), p. 13.

60. Statement before the House Ways and Means Committee, Washington, D.C., January 22, 1975, cited in *Department of Treasury News,* WS-200, p. 5.

61. The government fears a rise in inflation because it undermines the dollar in international trade, it distorts domestic investment into inflation-hedging ventures, and it creates the need for ever greater borrowing under conditions of extreme uncertainty as to future interest rates.

62. We do not, of course, think the analogy between an economic system and a machine is perfect. It traps the mind into a quest for simple, discrete variables, each with an independent, quantifiable effect. But the term fine tuning was introduced by the New Economists themselves, implying a machine that is basically in good repair.

Inequality, the American Way

Dimensions of Inequality

Income refers to the money returns from wages, gifts, and so on, that enable one to purchase goods. Wealth refers, in its broadest sense, to the market value of the property one owns; in a more restricted sense, it means the ownership of income-producing assets such as bonds and corporate stock. To understand a system of inequality, one must understand inequalities in both wealth and income. But inequalities in wealth are particularly important. For those with wealth can use it to create income directly, and they can also employ it as a power resource to protect or extend their high status and privileges.

In the United States the top 10 percent of income earners control 56 percent of the nation's wealth; the bottom 10 percent have negative wealth—debts that outstrip their ownership of property.[1] When we restrict our terms to the ownership of corporate stock, a singularly important source of control over productive resources, the concentration of wealth becomes even more apparent. One half of one percent of the adult population controls 33 percent or more of such private wealth, and the wealthiest 2 percent holds over two thirds of the nation's corporate stock. State and local bonds, mortgages, and notes are distributed a bit more broadly. But even when these interest-producing assets are included, 20 percent of the population controls 77 percent of the nation's private wealth.[2] Eighty percent of the population divides the remaining 23 percent of productive wealth among itself, and most of the available wealth represented in that figure consists of those interest-producing bonds and notes that enhance individual income but do not compare to corporate stock as a source of power. If the idea of class is to refer primarily to ownership of the means of production, then in America today the capitalist class, that is, the class with the capital, consists basically of 2 percent of the population. Perhaps another 15 to 20 percent can be viewed as junior partners in that class.

Significant, if less extreme, inequality in the distribution of income has persisted in the United States throughout the twentieth century. In 1910, for example, the top fifth of the population received about 46 percent of the nation's income and the bottom fifth received 8 percent; by 1972 those figures had become 41 percent and 5 percent, respectively. As Table 3-1 shows, the proportion of income received by each fifth of the population has remained remarkably stable since 1947.

These income statistics certainly underrepresent the income of the top fifth of the population, because they do not include capital gains receipts and because respondents regularly underreport in-

TABLE 3-1.   Percentage Share of Aggregate Income, Received by Each Fifth of Families, 1947–1972

	1947	1957	1967	1972
Poorest fifth	5.1	5.0	5.5	5.4
Second fifth	11.8	12.6	12.4	11.9
Middle fifth	16.7	18.1	17.9	17.5
Fourth fifth	23.2	23.7	23.9	23.9
Richest fifth	43.3	40.5	40.4	41.4
(Richest 5 percent)	17.5	15.8	15.2	15.9

Source: U.S. Bureau of the Census, *Current Population Reports,* Series P-60, No. 90 (December 1973), p. 5.

come from interest, dividends, and rentals.[3] Robert Pechman and Benjamin Okner, for example, estimate that in 1966 the actual money income of the top fifth was as high as 47.9 percent, and that of the bottom fifth as low as 3.7 percent.[4] These estimates, if correct for 1966, would remain relatively constant today. Finally, while the figures summarized so far cover pretax income, the posttax percentage of income of each income fifth is not substantially changed. Pechman and Okner conclude that "because there is so little difference in effective rates over most of the income distribution the tax system has very little effect on the relative distribution of income."[5]

Income distribution figures merely summarize the relative purchasing power of each fifth of the population. But there is a substantial connection between occupational affiliation and income level, and unequal purchasing power is therefore merely one dimension of the entire system of inequality. In the United States occupational categories form a hierarchy in which professional and managerial positions typically receive the highest incomes, followed by semi-professional, skilled or manual, routine white-collar, and unskilled manual occupations in roughly that order. Table 3-2 illustrates this ranking.

Table 3-2 indicates the connection between income level and occupational affiliation but probably understates it. First, it underreports nonsalary income by those in upper occupations. Second, since opportunities for advancement within the upper categories outstrip those in the lower categories and since the risk of periodic unemployment is significantly greater in the lower categories, the *lifetime earnings* (the only time span worthy of close attention) of the typical manager or professional and the typical laborer will be much more unequal than revealed here. Third, these categories fail to distinguish those working in the corporate system from those working in the market system; but, in fact, blue-collar workers in the former system tend to earn more than their counterparts in the market system. (The Department of Commerce defines its categories as if we lived in a market system, making interpretation of its data difficult for those who know better.)

When the connection between income distribution and the occupational hierarchy is established, several other dimensions of our stratified system become visible. Thus managers, professionals, and other technicians in the corporate system not only receive comparatively high incomes but their sick pay benefits, health insurance, pension plans, long-term economic security, expense accounts, clean and healthy working environments, degree of control over

TABLE 3-2. Occupational and Employment Status, by Head of Household, by Total Income, 1972

	Under $4000	$4000–6999	$7000–9999	$10,000–14,999	$15,000–24,999	$25,000 & above
Professional and technical	4%	7%	12%	26%	35%	17%
Managers and administrators	4	6	10	25	33	20
Sales workers	7	11	14	26	29	13
Craftsmen and kindred workers	4	10	18	35	29	4
Operatives	7	17	23	33	18	2
Clerical	8	20	23	29	18	3
Farmers and farm managers	22	22	19	18	15	4
Laborers, except farm	12	21	25	27	13	3
Service workers	22	23	19	20	14	2
Farm workers	34	32	19	15	8	1

Source: Adapted from *Current Population Reports,* Series P-60, No. 89 (July 1973), p. 22.

work schedules, roles in decision making, and status outstrip by far the benefits received by blue-collar workers in these areas. Similarly, blue-collar workers in the corporate system tend to fare better on most of these dimensions than their counterparts in the market system. The system of income inequality, then, is simply *one manifestation* of a complex of cumulative inequalities anchored in the occupational system. To think only of income distribution when appraising inequality is to divert attention away from the cumulative nature and institutional basis of the distribution system.

The importance of keeping the entire system of inequality in view can hardly be overemphasized. At the time the Ford Motor Company, for instance, announced a new program of preventive health care for its 4000 salaried headquarters employees to cut down the incidence of heart attacks, alcoholism, and other "stress-related ills," another study revealed that of 1266 poor households in Nashville, Tennessee, only 13 percent of those with health problems were receiving proper medical attention, 95 percent lacked proper dental care, 94 percent lacked a nutritious diet, and 50 percent lacked health insurance of any sort.[6] If the United States balanced its system of unequal income with equal access to health-care facilities for all citizens, the system of inequality would be somewhat less onerous than it is. But, in fact, our system of income inequality is merely an index of a cumulative system that bestows a vast range of privileges and benefits upon some segments of the population while it imposes the most painful burdens and risks on others. Our distribution system creates its own nobles, peasants, and paupers, and only failure to acknowledge that the occupational system is the backbone of the distribution system can hide that fact from those who study inequality.[7]

The Burdens of Inequality

Since the money income (in constant dollars) of those in each income fifth in 1972 was higher than that of those equivalently placed in the income hierarchy in, say, 1952, many observers have concluded that the absolute standard of living of each income group has significantly improved between 1952 and 1972; only its position relative to other groups has remained constant. Those at the lower levels of the income system may be worse off than today's rich, but they are better off than yesterday's poor. In the jargon of social science, they are not absolutely deprived, only relatively deprived.

There is some initial plausibility to such an interpretation. Thus 27 percent of the population had incomes of $4000 or less in 1952, while only 12 percent did in 1972. But we doubt that those in the bottom two fifths are actually much better off today than in 1952 (or some earlier date) despite definite increases in real money income. For the proponents of the theory of relative deprivation fail to take into account the changing costs of partaking of the services and institutions that prevail at different times in the development of a technological society. If a family's dollar income grows (that is, constant dollars controlled for inflation) while the luxuries of one era literally become the necessities of the next, the actual change in welfare over the intervening years cannot be captured by reading off increases in real money income.

In 1924 one could store food in an icebox because the iceman delivered ice regularly and because the corner store made it convenient to buy groceries on a daily basis. But today the iceman no longer delivers ice and the corner store has disappeared. The electric refrigerator has replaced the icebox as the available means of food storage, and the supermarket now makes weekly shopping the most convenient and least expensive way to acquire food. The refrigerator has become a household necessity, not merely because everybody habitually uses it, but because the food distribution system requires its use.

The shift from the icebox to the refrigerator merely symbolizes, of course, the changed social and economic context in which today's consumers must make choices. If cheap cuts of meat are no longer available in the supermarket (perhaps they are not profitable enough), I must buy the more expensive cuts. If the "consumer durables" of today, such as television sets, washing machines, hot water heaters, refrigerators, automobiles, and even houses, wear out faster than in a previous period, I must simply replace them more often at the going prices. If public transportation is unavailable, I must purchase a car to drive to work and to shop. If the risks and costs of automobile accidents are growing, I must purchase expensive automobile insurance. If cars are more complicated than in the past, I must pay to have them repaired rather than fixing them myself. If building codes, plumbing regulations, and electrical specifications required by law are too complicated for the handyman of yesterday to understand, I must hire specialists to install and repair these household systems. If the breakdown of extended kinship ties threatens to leave my offspring unprotected in the event of death or injury, I must buy life and disability insurance to provide for their security. If home heating costs are going up, I must buy home insulation. If crime is increasing, I must buy locks and police dogs and alarm systems to protect my family. If my children today must go to college in order to attain positions equivalent to the one I took as a high school graduate, I must try to pay their way through college.

These are just some of the ways in which systems of health care, transportation, schooling, security, food distribution, and household repair, which were introduced initially to meet the desires and budgets of middle- and high-income groups, can become necessities for lower-income groups living in the same society. What is for the affluent a new and better social service is often for the poor a new and costly regulation or necessity of life.

It is difficult to ascertain the exact effect of such changes in the prevailing system of social services on the welfare of lower- and moderate-income groups, but recent studies by the Bureau of Labor Statistics can give us some indication.[8] The Bureau calculates three hypothetical budgets, *lower level, intermediate level*, and *higher level*, for a family of four living in an urban area. In 1972, for instance, the lower budget was $7386, the intermediate $11,446, and the higher $16,558. According to the Bureau, the intermediate budget provides a "modest but adequate" standard of living: It enables the father to buy a new suit every two to four years, the mother to purchase one new coat every five years; the family to purchase a new refrigerator or stove every seventeen years, a used car every four years; the parents to attend a movie once every six weeks. It is not exactly a model budget in the affluent society. And it makes no provision for extended illness, unemployment, vacations, a college education for the children. These problems, plans, and obligations are assumed away, for the children are young and the father is healthy in this hypothetical family. The minimum budget is still more austere, merely providing minimal food, clothing, and housing for the family under optimistic assumptions about its health and the availability of the proper items. These two budgets are so high in dollar figures and so low in purchasing power, we think, at least partly because of the social services any family must acquire if it is to live in an urban or suburban area.

But even by these quite modest standards the American economy does not measure up very well. In 1972 only 30 percent of American families had incomes of $15,000 or more, meaning that 70 percent of the families fell below the higher-level budget. Half of the families in that category had two breadwinners, increasing their costs for transportation, babysitters, and so on. The median family income for that year was $11,120, slightly below the moderate budget required for an urban family of four. And 27 percent of the families had incomes of $7000 or less, placing them at or below the minimum-budget figure.[9] If the system of inequality in an economy of private corporations is justified on the grounds that it creates prosperity for the majority of the population, these figures must call that claim into question. For even during periods of economic expansion and of growth in the real-money income of most families, technology converts the luxuries of a previous generation into the necessities of the next. As a result, at least 40 percent of the families in America are struggling to make ends meet, even during periods of relative price stability. When inflation accelerates, that figure grows and the plight of those within that category deepens. It leads one to suspect that the New Economists like Arthur Okun are simply on the wrong track when they suggest that we must first expand production and employment and then cope with inequities built into the system.[10]

But the burdens of a stratified system are not sufficiently

catalogued even after we have identified the unequal chances for security, health care, recreation, education, fulfilling work life, and consumer goods that flow out of the system. The myth of equality of opportunity within a system of unequal rewards—the idea that individuals have a fair chance to move to significantly higher positions in society if they are especially energetic, intelligent, skilled, and lucky—contributes other injuries as well. Following the lead of Sennett and Cobb in their sensitive study, *The Hidden Injuries of Class*,[11] we can identify a series of traps faced by the low-income breadwinner seeking to serve the best interests of a family under adverse conditions.

People need to believe that they can play some role of importance in shaping their own lives, in living up to ideals and principles they accept in providing for the current welfare and future chances of their children. In a class system where people are classified and rewarded according to prevailing standards of worthiness, those at the lower end of the scale may deny in the abstract the validity of a system that first gives them lowly jobs and then blames them for being so lowly but, when one thinks about his own life, one tends to blame oneself, at least in part, for failure to climb further up the occupational ladder. Perhaps, the worker thinks, I did not apply myself enough in school or I am too stupid (and therefore deserving of low pay and status) or I have given in to the desire for a new car or a vacation rather than planning ahead. Perhaps I have done—or failed to do—any number of things that together explain why I remain near the bottom. The system of classification and differential reward, combined with the myth of equality of opportunity, generates self-doubt and self-reproach among those who stand at the lower levels of the stratification system. "If I hadn't quit school to make a fast buck, I wouldn't be where I am today," is the typical remark of a blue-collar worker in the Sennett and Cobb interviews.[12]

Partly to make up for that lingering sense of unworthiness, partly to ensure that the next generation can escape this plight, blue-collar employees often work long hours to give their children a chance to move up the occupational ladder. These workers are not primarily motivated by the goals that energize the "economic man" of mainstream economic theory; they are willing to sacrifice now so that their children will not have to experience the same hardships and low self-esteem in the future. But this motive, while effective from the point of view of the employer as an incentive to work, further complicates the life of the worker.

If the breadwinner is unsuccessful in helping the children escape, then the sacrifice has been all for nothing. If, on the other hand, success is attained, it will probably be at the expense of losing too much time away from the family in whose name the sacrifice was made. And if, as is very common, both parents work to promote their objective, that consequence is doubled. Moreover, if the progeny do move on to higher positions, their new geographic and class location will separate them from the parents. The very network of extended kinship ties which can provide solace and support to people suffering hardships is undermined by the mobility of the children. In our system working class parents can hardly help feeling ambivalent about the future of their children because, win or lose in the struggle to lift the next generation up, something of importance is lost.

To compete for the few promotion opportunities available, the worker must meet the expectations and attitudes of superiors more than fellow workers. So that once again, whereas losing the promotion can mean failure, winning it, the worker loses, too. For now the task is to enforce rules and policies previously experienced as a burden, against workers once identified with.

Sennett and Cobb help us to understand such hidden injuries of class inequality and to comprehend as well the intense resentment and hostility people in such positions often feel against both intellectuals and welfare recipients: They help us, that is, to see the forces at work which divide constituencies that would have to be united if the system of inequality were to be changed significantly. If the welfare recipient can get income and food even when unemployed, a central source of meaning in the worker's life has been nullified: a willingness to *sacrifice* for one's family no longer seems so necessary. Why then make the sacrifice? If intellectuals call for expanded welfare programs; if they "coddle" criminals; if they criticize consumerism, they in effect ridicule the sacrifices and goals which give meaning (are available as a source of meaning) for the workers. The system of inequality, supplemented by the myth of equality of opportunity, thus deepens the hardship of those at the lower levels while dividing them from others who are potential allies in opposing the system itself.

Apologies for Inequality: The Functionalist Theory

Each person, most of us believe, has the capacity to feel pain and experience satisfaction, to formulate and act upon personal projects, to enter into complex relationships of love, trust, resentment, friendship with others, to suffer grievously from the loss of a loved one, and to feel indignation if the dignity of another is improperly denied.

Since each of us has these capacities, we expect arrangements that undermine the satisfaction, projects, and dignity of some while magnifying those of others to receive some special justification. Why, we reasonably ask, are some placed so low while others are placed so high? Are those at the bottom lacking some of the characteristics we generally attribute to human beings? If so, that would constitute a justification; for we do not complain if someone fails to treat a worm like a person, only if someone treats a person like a worm. Or if it is not the lack of these human capacities that justifies inequality, is it perhaps to the benefit of the entire society to distribute rewards unequally?

It is useful to regard theories explaining inequality as efforts to answer these moral questions. Some theories explain inequality so as to justify the system sustaining it; others do so in ways that open the system to moral condemnation. It is appropriate to view the functionalist theory of inequality in this light. If the functionalist theory is basically sound, no sensible person would condemn the system that sustains inequality. The burdens it generates would be seen as necessary costs required to maintain a good society, just as we think of long practice as an essential prerequisite to becoming a concert pianist. To put it another way, to criticize the American system of inequality one must first show flaws in the functionalist theory, which is so often advanced to explain and justify those arrangements.[13]

A functionalist in social science is one who seeks to understand the operation of an institution like the family, government, religion, the market, or a class system by showing how each contributes to the maintenance of the larger social system within which it operates. Each institution is understood in terms of the *functions* it performs within the entire system. And some institutions, according to theorists of functionalism, are functionally imperative in all complex societies; no stable system can survive without them. Inequality is thought to be one such functional imperative of any complex society.

A succinct statement of the functionalist theory of inequality was presented some years ago by two sociologists, Kingsley Davis and Wilbert Moore.[14] Every society, they assert, must first distribute its members into the various jobs or roles defined by the society and then motivate them to perform their tasks efficiently. Some roles or positions are more important than others in the sense that the successful performance of them is crucial to the welfare of the whole society. In addition, some tasks require skills that are either difficult or scarce because they require a good deal of special training. In order to ensure that the most important and difficult tasks are performed competently, every society rewards the performance of these tasks highly. The system of unequal rewards thereby functions as a set of incentives to channel the most competent people into the most important and difficult roles and then ensures that they will perform these tasks efficiently. The greater the division of labor in society, the greater the range must be between the positions with the lowest rewards and those with the highest. "Social inequality," in the words of the authors, "is thus an unconsciously evolved device by which societies insure that the most important positions are conscientiously filled by the most qualified persons."[15]

The general theory, as stated, is incomplete. If you explain why my heart pumps blood by showing me that its function is to keep sufficient blood flowing through my body to maintain life, you have displayed the heart's role in maintaining my life but have not yet explained why it performs that function. We don't yet know why the heart works, only what work it does. Similarly, to claim that inequality places the most qualified people in the most important positions (its function) is not to explain how the system of inequality is created and maintained.

When they turn to this question, Davis and Moore explicitly deny that the power of some over others is the principal means by which inequality is maintained: "It should be stressed that a position does not bring power and prestige because it draws a high income. Rather it draws a high income because it is functionally important and the available personnel is for one reason or another scarce."[16] But then they shy away from stating explicitly why these functional requirements are met.

We can correct this omission by specifying an assumption often acknowledged by functionalists and surely implicit in the theory of Davis and Moore. (If this is not the correct assumption, we must be informed which one *is* and how it squares with the other dimensions of functionalist theory.) Stability, in a system where each position receives approximately the level of reward required to get the most qualified people into it and to motivate them to work conscientiously, is based on the *consent of the population*, or in the jargon of social science, on the consensus of beliefs and values accepted by the majority of the population. Acceptance of the established system of inequality is part of the consensus. The population comes to understand that inequality is functional; it comes to see that a system of unequal rewards works to the advantage of the whole system by ensuring that roles central to society's welfare are well carried out.

The population thus voluntarily accepts, or consents to, the system of inequality.

Put another way, a central tenet of the functionalist theory of inequality is that the population more or less tacitly comes to adopt that theory as part of its own understanding of established inequalities and to consent to established inequality because of that understanding. Thus, only if the participants were to accept another theory of inequality, one that finds the established inequalities unnecessary and exploitative, would it be necessary to employ large doses of coercive power to maintain the system. As long as the dominant ideology is functionalism we will have a consensus behind the system of inequality; if that ideology is challenged, the inequality must be maintained in some other way.

The functionalist explanation of inequality is deeply rooted in the traditions of American intellectual life. Thus James Madison, while laying out fundamental principles of the American Constitution in *Federalist No. 10*, expressed such views very clearly. The separation of powers, checks and balances, and division of powers between the states and the national government were designed to disperse and obstruct the power of those who might develop a "rage for paper money, for an abolition of debts, for an equal division of property, or any other improper or wicked project."[17] And Madison justified the unequal division of property in terms quite congenial to contemporary functionalists:

> From the protection of different and unequal faculties of acquiring property, the possession of different degrees and kinds of property immediately results; and from the influence of these on the sentiments and views of the respective proprietors ensues a division of society into different interests and parties.[18]

Madison was not as optimistic as modern functionalists that a consensus could be built around the established inequalities. He thought therefore that the "first object of government" was to protect the division of property, because the division itself was essential to the welfare of the system.

Today Milton Friedman holds that the market is the most efficient way of filling the most important posts with the most competent people and that equality of opportunity is the principle that allows the market to select the most competent individuals. Inequality of position, in a market system, reflects functional imperatives, and both the market and the inequality it sustains are supported by a broad social consensus: "No society can be stable unless there is a basic core of value judgments that are unthinkingly accepted by the great bulk of its members. I believe that payment in accordance with product has been, and in large measure still is, one of these accepted value judgments or institutions."[19]

Others who believe that the market is increasingly displaced by a rather benevolent corporate elite limited by labor, government, a broad consensus, and the conscience of its own managers, also conclude that the established system of inequality is basically sound. As one exponent of this view puts it, "The system is not equalitarian . . . nor probably should it be. Superior character, high ability, greater capacity to render those services which society needs not only can but should be rewarded more highly."[20]

Many writers in a variety of fields accept the functionalist theory of inequality, and they are ready to draw the appropriate moral conclusion: If inequality works to the advantage of the whole system, it should be maintained. What other view could one reasonably hold *if* the functionalist theory is correct?

The theory, however, is open to telling criticisms, criticisms which do not destroy it completely but which radically narrow the range of inequalities that can be justified as functional imperatives.

1. While it is usually easy enough to tell which skills are in scarce supply, it is not so easy to tell which tasks are the most important to the welfare of a particular society. Garbage collection is terribly important today, probably more important than, say, advertising detergents, writing comic strips, or selling used cars. But is it as important as managing a corporation, teaching young children, psychoanalyzing public officials? How would one decide? In practice, functionalists shift from assessing the relative *importance* of any particular position to assessing its relative *skill* level and the *scarcity* of that skill in the population. Fortunately for them, the skills required to psychoanalyze public officials are more scarce today than those required to collect garbage.

2. Scarcity of needed skills becomes the primary test, then, but if a profession is strategically located in a restricted market economy, it can do much to make sure that the supply of skilled personnel in its profession is limited. It thereby ensures its practitioners a high income. This is surely why doctors are paid so highly. The profession limits the supply of physicians through control over entry to medical schools and then, through the American Medical Association, lobbies government effectively to make sure that physicians do not lose the right to set fees privately. The *market power* of the medical

profession is surely a better explanation of its very high income level than is the functionalist interpretation of its position offered by Davis and Moore: "Modern medicine, for example, is within the mental capacity of most individuals, but a medical education is so burdensome and expensive that virtually none would undertake it if the position of the M.D. did not carry a reward commensurate with the sacrifice."[21]

It is plausible to explain much of the expense of medical education, the small number and size of medical schools, even the length of medical education as artifacts of unionized control over access to the profession rather than as necessary features of medical practice. Similar points apply to lawyers, accountants, skilled crafts, and so on. *Once the first criterion of the functionalists—functional importance—recedes to the background, the functionalist interpretation of the second—scarcity of needed skills—becomes very problematic.*

3. Functionalists emphasize the affirmative side of their theory—the need to identify scarce talent and to motivate those who possess it to work efficiently. But if their assumptions about human motivation are correct, there is another side to functionalist theory as well. Since those at the lower end of the income stream cannot be motivated by high rewards, they must be motivated by such "incentives" as the belief, whether true or false, that a good performance will be rewarded with promotion, the fear of unemployment, the need to provide for a family even under the most adverse circumstances. And as workers at the bottom get older, the first incentive must give way to the others. Only then will it be possible, on functionalist assumptions, to ensure that the most dangerous, demeaning, dirty, and routinized jobs are "conscientiously filled by the most qualified persons." High income cannot be the incentive, for according to the theory, low income at this level must provide the differential needed to fill the higher positions with qualified and conscientious workers. It should be no coincidence, then, from the vantage point of functionalist theory, that not only low income but poverty, unemployment, and the continual threat of unemployment are concentrated among those jobs where the skill level is the lowest and the supply of skills the greatest. These threats are the functional requirements of a stratified society. They ensure a supply of menial workers at low cost to the society. And these agents often supply service at low cost to high-income personnel, rewarding the latter even more for performance of their skilled tasks. It is a beautiful

theory (and system) when all its assumptions are spelled out: The carrot at higher levels *requires* the stick at lower levels.

4. The functionalists assume that the incentives to work that prevail in our society must prevail in every society. In that respect the theory is quite close to classical and neoclassical economic theory. But it could be that inequality in our society is so great in part because work in our society is organized basically around *external* and *individual* incentives. An external incentive is one, like money, that stands outside the work process itself. It is in contrast to an internal incentive, such as the fulfilling or challenging nature of the task. An individual incentive is in contrast to a shared incentive, as when the work itself involves fulfilling social relationships (an internal, social incentive) or when the object of work will be a contribution to some collectivity with which one identifies. It seems likely that a broader mix of external, individual, internal, and social incentives is *possible* in the organization of a society's division of labor. If so, it could be that our system of inequality is functional relative to the division of labor and incentive forms we have developed. But then our system of inequality would not reflect universal functional imperatives, but the imperatives of our particular system of production and work. And that would really amount to a refutation of functionalist theory: It would point toward reform of our system of production and work so as to relieve (among other things) the burdens of inequality. Why should we tolerate those burdens if they are remediable? The answer to that question also reveals why functionalist theory must view the incentive system prevailing in our society as the incentive system of society per se.

5. For the system of inequality to operate smoothly, a majority of the population must see it as the functionalist theorists see it—as working to benefit the entire society. And most of the members of the system must also believe that their assigned roles and reward levels reflect their abilities and the relative value of their services to the society. When these conditions are met, the stratified system will rest upon a consensus; even those at the lower levels will understand that the threat of unemployment is needed to keep them working. But if these conditions are met, only those at the higher levels can *both* believe in the system and have a sense of self-esteem. (Those who accept functionalist theory wholeheartedly tend to be clustered near the upper end of the income stream). The others must see themselves as at least partly responsible for their own lowly fate. My incompetence, laziness, or lack of discipline are responsible

for my low position and for the restricted life chances of my children. In this way, acceptance of (popularized versions of) functionalist theory becomes one of the burdens of class. It generates exactly the shame and self-doubt Sennett and Cobb identified as the hidden injuries of class.

An Alternative Theory of Inequality

The factors that explain the historical development of an institution do not necessarily explain how it is maintained today. Thus if members of a village select and follow a leader during a siege, his position emerges through community consent. But if, after the siege is over, he uses the resources at his disposal to retain his position even against opposition, his position of preeminence is now based on his exercise of power over his followers.

We will argue that an expanding and powerful industrial elite played a crucial role in creating the structure of inequality that prevails today. One of the effects of this process was to allow an accumulation of capital for further industrial expansion; another was to push the industrial working class into a subordinate and precarious economic position. Now that the system of inequality is solidified, the corporate elite continues to play some continuing role in its maintenance. But the stability of the system itself is further enhanced because the system of inequality itself divides groups that would have to be united if the system were to be altered. Each subordinate group, to put it starkly, is both exploited and a willing or unwilling participant in the exploitation of others. The result, in broadest outline, is a stable hierarchy, graded by power, in which every "new pressure or imposition moves along the line of least resistance which, though not in its first stage, usually and eventually runs in a descending direction." And, as Georg Simmel, the author of this imagery, reminds us, the pressure in such a structure of inequality flows inexorably downward until it reaches those at the bottom:

> This is the tragedy of whoever is the lowest. . . . He not only has to suffer from the deprivations, efforts, and discriminations which, taken together, characterize his position; in addition every new pressure on any point whatever in the superordinate layers is, if technically possible at all, transmitted downward and stops only at him.[22]

We begin by considering briefly the development of the modern wage-labor system in one industry—the steel industry—around the turn of the century. The pressures at work in that industry existed in other basic industries, too, and the outlines of our modern corporate system, and the system of inequality attached to it, were created.

Before 1892 the production of steel required a group of highly skilled craftsmen who held a strategic position in the production system. "At every point rollers, roughers, and heaters had manually handled the metal. They were men of long experience and at a premium in America."[23] These craftsmen would negotiate a fixed rate of pay per unit of production with management and then "contract out" wages to semiskilled and unskilled workers who worked for them.[24] If the skilled workers were dissatisfied with working conditions or with their pay scales, they could strike until management was ready to negotiate. For when the members of the Amalgamated Association, the union of steel craftsmen, went on strike, there were no skilled craftsmen to replace them.

But as the market for steel expanded and as new technologies allowed pig iron (the crude iron from which steel is made) to be produced faster than finished steel, the steel owners saw possibilities for new profits in the mechanization of the entire process. Moreover, if they could create a process in which every required skill could be easily acquired, and therefore every skilled worker could be replaced easily, they could gain more control over the work force. They could then set wage rates that seemed appropriate to them, regulate the conditions of work, and discipline or fire stubborn workers. They could do all this by developing a production system in which no group of workers possessed scarce and indispensable skills.

The Carnegie Company, with Andrew Carnegie at the helm, had both these objectives in mind when it set the stage for the classic steel strike of 1892 in Homestead, Illinois. As a partner in the Carnegie Corporation said, "The Amalgamated placed a tax on improvements, therefore the Amalgamated had to go."[25]

Henry Clay Frick, the chief executive of Carnegie's operation, prepared carefully for the 1892 strike. He converted the factory into an armed fortress, hired three hundred Pinkerton detectives, and then announced that the company would no longer recognize the union but would negotiate with each worker individually. The Amalgamated then called a strike. After dozens of deaths, the intervention of the state militia, Pinkerton detectives, scabs, and the courts on the side of the company, the union was finally broken. Several consequences followed:

1. Blacks from the South, driven north by repression and increasing unemployment in their home states, were employed as strikebreakers.[26] This created deep animosity between white and black workers, neither group comprehending (or able to consider) the plight faced by the other. Similar incidents in future labor-management conflicts, plus the fact that the blacks when eventually given regular employment in the steel factories held the most debilitating and low-paying jobs, helped to divide these two segments of the labor force from one another. This historical development, rather than some hypothetical racism indigenous to blue-collar workers, fostered the persistence of racial conflict within the working class.

2. With the Amalgamated Association broken, the owners were able to mechanize the production of steel. Output was soon increased, the number of working hours was expanded to ten or twelve hours per day (often seven days a week), and work skills were defined so that no group of workers became indispensable to the enterprise. The system was structured so that managers did almost all of the *thinking, organizing* and *commanding* while the workers *monitored* specific pieces of machinery or did other *physical* work. Craftsmanship was thus replaced by labor in the steel industry. And while production increased rapidly during the next ten years, wage rates increased only modestly. "The accomplishment was possible," according to historian David Brody, "only with a labor force powerless to oppose the decisions of the steel men."[27]

3. Despite a significant reduction in the range of skills required for steel production, management soon found that a hierarchical system of wages, a set of "job ladders," was needed to motivate men to work efficiently and to weaken their ability to unite in organized opposition to management policies. As one manufacturer himself explained it in the early 1920s:

> When all are paid one rate, it is the simplest and most inevitable thing for all to unite in the support of a common demand. When each worker is paid according to his record there is not the same community of interest. . . . There are not likely to be union strikes when there is no union of interest.[28]

By *record* the manufacturer meant less the levels of skill of the workers than their attendance, their cooperation with management, the pace at which they worked, their opposition to unionism, and their willingness to accept overtime. The "job ladders" became a device for controlling workers while increasing their efficiency. Some of those who played the game by the new rules were pushed up the ladder while the others stayed behind. The result was to further divide workers from one another and thereby to make them and the wage rates they received easier to control. As the new system matured, one steelworker described the difficulties it presented to those who sought to organize a new union: "Naw they won't join the union; they're all after every other feller's job."[29] The "equality of opportunity," operating within the job ladders, focused each worker's attention on his chances for individual promotion and away from the risky possibilities for collective improvement of the position of the working class.

4. The migration of Slovaks, Poles, Croats, Serbs, Magyars, and Italians, encouraged by United States immigration policies and depressed economic conditions in Eastern Europe, swelled the labor force, weakened the possibilities for collective organization because of an available supply of labor to replace strikers, and created division and resentment amongst the various ethnic groups as each new wave found jobs below the groups that had migrated ahead of it. Since many of the immigrants came without wives and planned to return to the homeland as soon as possible, they were often willing to work hard for low pay. They usually avoided the established workers, who viewed them as a threat to their job security. The immigrants themselves often had few illusions about America. Letters to the homeland often concurred with the judgment of a Hungarian churchman: "Wherever the heat is the most insupportable, the flames the most scorching, the smoke and soot the most choking, there we are certain to find compatriots bent and wasted with toil."[30] The immigrants suffered, and the pay rates of the workers who had arrived before them were depressed by the new supply of labor. All this increased conflict within the working class, intersecting with the racial conflicts already present. When labor conflicts emerged again in the 1920s, corporate owners exploited these conflicts by playing one ethnic group off against others.

Our thesis is this: Once management, through its destruction of the old craft union and craft system of work, had introduced the new factory system, the system itself developed self-perpetuating tendencies. The job ladders, the principle of advancement through individual effort, the ethnic divisions, the replaceability of unskilled and semiskilled workers, the technology adapted to the needs of management control, the continuing flow of new labor into the region—all these forces divided workers and allowed corporate owners, always with the willing assistance of the state, to break efforts at collective organization with a minimum of difficulty. What emerged was not a functional system of inequality (the workers did not consent to it voluntarily; it was not the only possible way to organize production, to accumulate capital rationally, or to motivate workers to work; and it benefited some groups unnecessarily at severe cost to others). It was (and is) a hierarchical system of exploitation in which each occupational level is exploited, though to different degrees; each participates, often unwittingly, in the exploitation of the groups below it. Employers gained the loyalty of top managers, professionals, middle-level technicians and foremen first by paying them highly and providing job security, later by recruiting most of them not from inside the factory but from universities, where they are socialized to congenial values and expectations. The "loyalty" of the others was retained through job ladders with uniformly low wage ceilings, corporate welfare, and job insecurity.

This pattern was duplicated, with important variations of course, in each of the basic industries (roughly in what Galbraith calls the corporate or planning system). It is important to see that the successful organization of industrial trade unions in the 1930s occurred well after the basic consolidation of the industrial system of private corporations. The trade union leadership did not challenge the established pattern of private ownership, the structure of work, the distribution of income between workers and managers, even (much) the established balance between privately incorporated production for private consumption (depending upon private income level) and the social provision of public goods (energy, health care, transportation systems, public life insurance). The trade unions did introduce a measure of job security through seniority rules, press for social security and other retirement benefits, establish a system of due process for workers treated arbitrarily by management, and most important for the purposes of our inquiry, redistribute income within the working class.

Galbraith's thesis that our economy is marked by a subordinate market system (service industries, farming) and a dominant corporate system is pertinent to the question of how unions help to redistribute income within the working class and how they often unwittingly contribute to inequality and divisions within the working class. Established industrial unions in the United States have never challenged the right of corporate owners to make investment decisions, relocate, set prices, or determine the basic form of the assembly line. So when these unions demand higher wages for workers, corporate owners can comply and then raise prices to more than cover the increased wage costs. The cost of living then goes up, taking some of the wage gains away. But workers in the market system, who are seldom organized into unions and for whom unions cannot have much leverage even when they are organized, then find their cost of living has gone up also. Their employers are restricted by market competition and, most important, by the necessity of conforming to the terms of trade set by the large corporations who buy many of their products. Workers in the market system, then, cannot match the cost of living increase with an equivalent wage increase. In effect, the wage increase of the organized workers in the corporate system contributes to the higher cost of living faced by workers in the market system.

Functionalist theory is not completely wrong; it is just radically overstated by its proponents. And this overstatement unjustifiably legitimates an extreme inequality in the distribution of wealth, income, working conditions, job satisfaction, job security, health care, pension plans, and other fringe benefits that has persisted for decades and that stratifies the population in roughly the following order: corporate owners, market entrepreneurs, managers and professionals in both systems, white-collar workers in the corporate system, skilled manual workers in the corporate system and selected market areas, clerical workers in the market system, unskilled workers in the corporate system, unskilled workers in the market system. Our alternative interpretation, we suggest, accounts for the stability of this stratification system in terms of a complex set of political controls and divisive pressures within the production system. It also undermines the legitimacy of established inequalities, lending legitimacy to those who would reduce their scope.[31]

The Poverty of Liberal Reforms

In 1875 Karl Marx criticized those "vulgar socialists" who sought to reform the system of *distribution* while leaving the system of *production* basically intact:

> *Vulgar socialism (and from it in turn a section of democracy) has taken over from the bourgeois economists the consideration and treatment of distribution as independent of the mode of production and hence the presentation of socialism as turn-*

ing principally on distribution. . . . The distribution of the means of consumption at any time is only a consequence of the distribution of the conditions of production themselves.[32]

That criticism applies today to liberals who seek to redistribute income through government programs and yet are eager to leave the system of work and ownership intact. Their programs can at most result in very modest success; at worst they will fail miserably (remember the "war on poverty") and play into the hands of corporate conservatives, who have insisted all along that these programs cannot succeed.

Liberal proposals have included job training for the unemployed, expansion of welfare programs, a negative income tax to provide income floors for those at the bottom of the system, and most ambitiously, a graduated income tax that would significantly close the gap between high- and low-income earners. All of these proposals, it must be emphasized, leave the system of ownership and production untouched. They seek to reform the system of distribution without altering the system of production in which it is anchored.

The first problem with these proposals (though they are not unique in this respect) is that they are unlikely to receive the support of a majority of the electorate in the existing political economy. It goes almost without saying that the most powerful interest groups in the system will oppose the most ambitious of these reform proposals. But more is involved.

It is easier in our system of political economy to build an electoral majority of 51 percent from the top down than from the bottom up, because the top has more benefits to dispense to the middle than the bottom does. Not only is the blue-collar work force divided from within by the forces we have described, but corporate elites have impressive resources available in the prevailing system to maintain the loyalty of managerial and professional employees by providing them with high salaries and special benefits. These groups together can also align themselves politically with entrepreneurs, white-collar workers, and sometimes skilled blue-collar workers over a broad range of issues. Thus they can coalesce to protect or extend tax breaks for each group; to promote those military expenditures that provide investment and employment opportunities for each group; to provide public support for technical education so that corporate employment needs are financed through public funds and so that all taxpayers contribute to a system that primarily benefits children of middle- and upper-middle-class taxpayers; and so on.

During normal times, then, an electoral majority is easier to create from the top down than from the bottom up. This is largely because of the power of corporate elites to dispense benefits directly to potential allies and to play an important indirect role in securing benefits from government favorable to the same constituencies. Divisions, struggles, hard feelings certainly do emerge within these loosely forged coalitions, especially between its fringe members at lower occupational levels and its core members. But as George McGovern demonstrated in his 1972 campaign effort to redistribute income modestly through the tax system, these squabbles are ignored when class interests in the existing system of income distribution are at issue. This difficulty applies, of course, to other strategies for redistribution, too, but it is a decisive obstacle to those liberals who seek to achieve significant tax reforms through government while leaving the basic system of ownership and production intact.

Suppose, however, that the situation were to change (perhaps an economic crisis opened up new coalition possibilities) and liberals were able to push through a highly progressive income tax combined with an income floor while leaving everything else in the system intact. The reforms simply would not take. We would have to expect American investors to divert a larger portion of their investments abroad. American corporations with a multinational capability already established would also move part of their production abroad, where higher profits are possible. Workers at the bottom of the occupational hierarchy would loaf on the job (there is no reform of work life, remember; many of those who had to choose between deadening, demeaning work and a somewhat lower income without work would choose the latter—and rationally so). The demand for a range of private consumption goods previously reserved for the middle class would increase (remember that there is no shift from private goods to collective goods) just at the time production was lagging; and thus inflation would accelerate. The reforms, in short, would fail, and very soon a militant top-down coalition would organize to restore the old system of inequality. Egalitarian policies, having failed, would once again get a bad name, and the ideal of equality would lose a place on the liberal agenda for another generation.

The failure must be expected because the established system of inequality is largely *functional*, not in the universal sense claimed by functionalists, but as it operates in a historically specific system of private ownership, instrumental organization of work, and production oriented primarily to private consumption. Reform in these latter areas is an essential part of any meaningful effort to reduce inequality.

More specifically, two major structural changes are required to open the way for a reduction in inequality:

1. The system of production for private profit and private consumption (think of cars, individual houses, fashionable clothes) must increasingly be displaced by one of public ownership and the production of collective goods. Mass transit systems, health centers, recreation centers, schools are goods that can be made available to any citizen. To the extent that these collective goods become established in various spheres of life, the effective scope of inequality will be reduced.

2. The system of work must be reformed so that, first, more jobs become fulfilling in their own right, and second, those necessary jobs that are not open to such reform become increasingly the part-time responsibility of all able-bodied members of the society, whatever their major occupations. These reforms will lessen the need for extreme pay differentials as an incentive to work, and they will have the important direct effect of reducing the extreme inequality of working conditions. Of course, these reforms will also require public ownership of the means of production; private owners will not accept meaningful reform voluntarily because, as the earlier example of the old craft unions in the steel industry made clear, meaningful work reform erodes the ability of private owners to control the productive system in their private interests.[33]

These reforms are not in principle unachievable. There is no technological imperative that makes their implementation impossible. They are, of course, unacceptable to major interests in the system and unfamiliar to many citizens who would benefit from them. But the political obstacles to such reduction in inequality are not in themselves an argument against our theory of inequality or our proposals for change; rather they reflect the inadequacy of the system that obstructs such programs. The first move toward revising that system is to deny its beneficiaries the ideological cover, that is, the ideology of functionalism within a market system, that has previously justified an oppressive, exploitative system of inequality.

There are some signs that the pressures to reduce inequality will emerge with renewed force during the next decade. First, the ethnic divisions within the work force that traditionally have weakened working-class unity have declined in importance today. Also, an increasing number of workers are aware that not all countries organize work and income incentives the way we do; they are less easily convinced today that the established ways are the only ways. Finally, as the economic system faces increasing pressures from resource depletion, environmental decay, growing international constraints, internal inflation, unemployment, and a population overeducated for the jobs available, we can expect an increase in labor unrest. Since many of these constraints set limits to the old ideal of an indefinitely expanding economy, with its promise of growth in money income for most workers, the pressures to divide the existing pie more equitably are likely to grow more intense.

It is not clear how successful renewed pressure for a reduction in inequality can be. But even if immediate success were marginal, a social movement organized around these objectives would still be worthwhile. As we have seen, one of the hidden injuries of class is the low self-esteem that typically accompanies a low-class position. Those who even partly accept the functionalist ideology internalize an ethic that places blame on themselves for the burdens they and their children bear. Acceptance of an alternative ideology, which locates the structural sources of inequality within the established political economy, would externalize that responsibility; it would thus help to lift a burden of shame that has unjustifiably been projected onto the victims of the established system. This process of externalization is important in itself; it is also essential to the development of a political movement for equality.

Finally, since acceptance of a radical theory of inequality places liberal schemes for redistribution in critical perspective, it also enables the left to dissociate itself from those redistributive programs doomed to fail in the present system. It thereby helps to maintain a good name for equality even while the misconceived egalitarian schemes of liberals falter.

NOTES

1. *Business Week* (August 5, 1972).
2. See Ferdinand Lundberg, *The Rich and the Super Rich* (New York: Bantam Books, 1969), ch. 1.
3. See *Current Population Reports*, Series P-60, No. 89 (July 1973), p. 3. The income of the bottom fifth might be underrepresented too, since respondents often underreport income from public assistance and social security.
4. *Who Bears the Tax Burden?* (Washington, D.C.: Brookings Institution, 1974), p. 46.
5. Ibid., p. 6.
6. The Ford plan was announced in *Business Week*, June 8, 1974, p. 24.

The Nashville study is summarized in the *New York Times*, October 23, 1974, p. 88.

7. For further discussion of the connection between income inequality and the occupational system, see Frank Parkin, *Class Inequality and Political Order* (New York: Praeger Publishers, 1971).

8. See *Three Standards of Living for an Urban Family of Four Persons*, Bulletin 1570-51, Bureau of Labor Statistics (Spring 1967), and *Urban Family Budget Updated to Autumn 1972*, Bureau of Labor Statistics, Vol. 96, No. 8.

9. *Current Population Reports*, Series P-60, No. 90 (December 1973); data are taken from pages 3, 4, and 27. These figures do not correspond perfectly with the budget levels set by the Bureau of Labor Statistics. The figures cover both rural and urban families and the family sizes vary (two-person 37 percent, three-person 21 percent, four-person 20 percent, five-person or more 23 percent). But these discrepancies are surely compensated for by the fact that the Bureau budget assumes an established couple married fifteen years, a nonworking wife, children not yet of college age, and the absence of serious health problems or accidents.

10. See *The Political Economy of Prosperity* (New York: Norton, 1970), especially pp. 123–125.

11. (New York: Random House, 1973).

12. *The Hidden Injuries of Class*, p. 187.

13. More developed discussions of the connections between explanatory theory and normative judgment can be found in Charles Taylor, "Neutrality in Political Science," and William Connolly, "Theoretical Self-Consciousness," in *Social Structure and Political Theory*, ed. William Connolly and Glen Gordon (Lexington, Mass.: Heath, 1974), pp. 16–39 and pp. 40–68.

14. "Some Principles of Stratification," *American Sociological Review* (April 1945), pp. 242–249. Reprinted in Connolly and Gordon. Quotations are taken from this book of readings.

15. Ibid., p. 114.

16. Ibid., p. 119.

17. *Federalist No. 10* (Indianapolis: Bobbs Merrill, 1954), p. 19.

18. Ibid., p. 12.

19. Milton Friedman, *Capitalism and Freedom* (Chicago: University of Chicago Press, 1962), pp. 166–167.

20. Adolf Berle, *Power Without Property* (New York: Harcourt, Brace and World, 1959), p. 145.

21. Davis and Moore, "Some Principles of Stratification," p. 115.

22. Quoted in Kurt H. Wolff (ed.), *The Sociology of Georg Simmel* (New York: Free Press, 1950), pp. 236–37.

23. David Brody, *Steelworkers in America: The Non-Union Era* (New York: Harper and Row, 1960), pp. 31–32.

24. Actually, the contracting system was more complex and variable

than presented here, but the complexities do not affect our thesis. For further information, see Katherine Stone, "The Origin of Job Structures in the Steel Industry," *Review of Radical Economics* (Summer 1974), pp. 113–174. Our presentation of developments in this industry are indebted to her essay, to the above study by Brody, and to Jeremy Brecher, *Strike!* (Greenwich, Conn.: Fawcett Publications, 1974).

25. Brody, p. 54.
26. The double bind of the black workers, driven from the south and despised in the north by whites whose jobs they threatened, is explored sensitively by Stanley Aronowitz, *False Promises: The Shaping of American Working Class Consciousness* (New York: McGraw Hill and Co., 1973), esp. ch. 3.
27. Brody, pp. 48–49.
28. Stone, p. 131 (our emphasis).
29. Ibid., p. 134.
30. Brody, p. 99.
31. A complete account would include more detailed discussion of women, elderly, the chronically unemployed, the infirm. We simply want to suggest here that these categories, important in their own right and to a thorough picture of the stratification system, can be comprehended to a great extent through the occupational categories that set the crucial terms within which inequality operates. The occupational system is the fundamental dimension of the system of stratification, though it alone is not sufficient to full understanding of it.
32. Marx, *Critique of the Gotha Programme* (1875) (New York: International Publishers, 1970), pp. 10, 11.
33. The reduction of inequality, it should be noted, does not necessarily require the elimination of all job ladders in specific occupations, although the difference between the top and bottom levels *between* occupations must be reduced greatly. If younger workers earn less than middle-aged workers within an occupation, this is not an inegalitarian practice unless the younger workers cannot expect eventually to move to those higher levels. It is not equality in any particular year that counts, but equality over a lifetime.

Nature and Its Largest Parasite

Ecology deals with the balance between organisms and their environment—between human beings and nature. The issues posed by such a relationship touch the very survival of humanity on the planet Earth. We depend on nature for air to breathe, soil to grow food, water to drink and to sustain vegetation, fossil fuels to provide heat and to power the production system, metals to provide material for commodities. But if nature is our host we are its parasites. We abuse it unmercifully, robbing it of nonrenewable materials, straining its self-restorative capacities.

If some economic systems are more parasitical than others, the structure of that

Parts of this chapter are drawn from "Market Images and Corporate Power: Beyond the 'Economics of Environmental Management,'" by Michael H. Best and William E. Connolly, in *Public Policy Evaluation*, ed. Kenneth M. Dolbeare, Vol. II of *The Yearbooks in Politics and Public Policy*, Copyright 1975, pp. 41–74. By permission of the publisher, Sage Publications, Inc.

relationship, and the problems it spawns, must be confronted before the host collapses from the strain. This is particularly pertinent today. For as corporate capitalism, the ultimate ecoparasite by any measure of resource use or waste disposal, faces a new round of internal crises, ecology is apt to lose its popularity as a political issue. Such a lapse must be challenged, because the current maladies of the system are partly rooted in a long-term debt to nature that is coming due.

Any reasonable assessment of the policy sciences in America must account for the lag between the escalation of ecological assault and its recognition by social scientists. Respected textbooks in political science and economics written before 1965 paid little heed to the issue. The social costs of environmental misuse became a national disgrace before they became the serious object of policy analysis by mainstream social scientists.[1]

Perhaps, though, the omission looks like a deficiency of theory only by hindsight. Perhaps the adverse environmental effects of the political economy of corporate capitalism were until recently too unobtrusive to be captured within the conceptual net of any intellectual system. Unfortunately, the earlier work of two maverick social scientists, K. William Kapp, an economist, and Grant McConnell, a political scientist, suggests that this is not true.[2] Their intellectual frameworks allowed them to detect abuses of nature resulting from prevailing forms of production and consumption even while these connections remained obscure to those trapped within the categories of pluralist political and neoclassical economic theory. In *The Social Costs of Private Enterprise* (1950), Kapp documents the

> *destructive effects of air and water pollution . . . [and] occupational diseases . . . , the competitive exploitation of both self-renewable and exhaustible natural wealth such as wildlife, petroleum and coal reserves, soil fertility and forest resources . . . ; the diseconomies of the present transport system.*[3]

These social costs had gone unnoted and untended, according to Kapp, because they "do not enter into the cost calculations of private firms." And economists failed to detect them, too, not because they indulged in "wilful apologetics" for the private enterprise system, but because "the phenomena of social costs" seems to "have no room in the conceptual system of traditional value and price analysis."[4] Particularly important, he thought, was the faulty attempt by his professional colleagues to separate economic from political analysis, as if each could be treated as a distinct system. The ironic outcome of such an effort was a set of assumptions and concepts that maintained an unacknowledged and thus undefended "union between economic analysis and political liberalism."[5]

McConnell's early analysis of the political obstacles facing any conservation movement was built upon ideas quite similar to Kapp's. He castigated pluralist political scientists for their refusal to see that compromises among organized private interests often produced results harmful to the public interest (his corollary to Kapp's idea of the social costs of private transactions). He criticized them for their failure to identify the corporation as "the most important form of private government in America today" and particularly for their continued acceptance of the "historic liberal" image of "an autonomous economy and its corollary, an autonomous politics."[6]

The prescience of Kapp and McConnell would be merely of historical interest (and academic embarrassment) amid the universal attention given to environmental issues today except for one further development. Adopting ideas very much like those Kapp and McConnell thought had blinded their predecessors to the environmental impact of the American political economy, contemporary policy scientists today purport to have a program to restore environmental integrity while retaining the autonomy of the market economy.

In contemporary America policy scientists who perceive the economy as a competitive market system invariably see pluralism as its mirror image in politics. Indeed, since pluralist theory is basically market theory transposed to politics, we can say that each image is a mirror to the other: If one is blurred, the other will shift out of focus also. We will argue that the assumptions and policy priorities of social scientists who favor market images of the economy and polity are still disconnected today from the very environmental problems their predecessors failed to detect yesterday. Only an analysis linking private consumerism and industrial waste to our system of power, product designs, work life incentives, and economic inequality can account adequately for the dangerous imbalance between human beings and nature that results from the political economy of corporate capitalism.

The Market Model of Environmental Management

The market, according to neoclassical theorists, is still a sound mechanism for coordinating economic transactions. But there are more and more *unpriced* effects of market transactions that must be incorporated into the market's pricing system. Air, water, and soil pollution are not automatically translated into market costs because the environmental effects of particular economic transactions are diffused over a wide population and to some extent projected onto future populations. Under such circumstances it is irrational for any individual producer or consumer to accept voluntarily the higher costs involved in curtailing pollution of the environment. Thus a company that purifies the water used in production before disposing it into streams adds to its own costs, fails to benefit from the purified water flowing downstream, and weakens its competitive market position with respect to those companies unwilling to institute purification procedures. Since it is reasonable to assume that other companies in a market system will not voluntarily weaken their position in this way, it is irrational for any single company to choose to do so. The same logic applies to the consumer who assesses the rationality of, say, placing an emission control device on the automobile exhaust system.

Thus practices that are desirable from the viewpoint of the public are irrational from the viewpoint of any particular consumer or producer. And policies that are rational for individual consumers and producers go against the collective interest in preserving nonrenewable productive resources and maintaining the environment's capacity to assimilate wastes. This is the "tragedy of the commons."[7]

To cope with this problem most economists think the government should establish by law a system of charges and subsidies; the adverse side effects of market transactions are then priced high enough to make it economical for producers and consumers to conserve nonrenewable energy resources and to establish waste disposal systems that preserve the purity of air, water, and soil. As a secondary bonus, the new system of prices stimulates private business to produce improved disposal and recycling facilities, since there is now profit in such enterprises. Much recent environmental legislation is based on this theory.

We do not say that such a program is inherently irrational. For any viable environmentalist program must somehow find a way to incorporate environmental costs into economic transactions. But if such a scheme were really to work, it would require basic alterations in the system of political economy. We will first identify some problems internal to the market theory and then turn to an alternative interpretation that places such a pricing system in a quite different context.

First, it is not at all clear that the intrusion of politics into the marketplace on the massive scale required to "internalize the externalities" would not create severe dislocations in the delicate, self-adjustive market mechanisms. Certainly a huge bureaucracy is required to identify the environmental costs of so many production processes and waste disposal systems and to administer a tax and subsidy program reflecting these assessments.

Moreover, the problems of measuring and assessing environmental costs become magnified when considering costs to future generations. What will motivate today's voters, many of whom are treated unjustly within the prevailing economic system, to incorporate by law the needs and claims of future generations into current market transactions? Why should proponents of this model, who assume that individuals are inherently self-interested, think that current generations will be willing to build the interests of future generations into the pricing system?[8]

Finally, a market system that retains private control of the investment and pricing functions requires continued economic growth as a spur to investment. But a point may well be reached when growth itself is incompatible with environmental imperatives. Some experts believe, for instance, that a steady rate of growth will eventually (within several generations) generate atmospheric heat levels incompatible with human life.[9] Many suspect that other factors, such as the depletion of key resources before adequate substitutes are found, will force an end to, or a profound slowdown of, economic growth. The ecological effects of economic processes are often delayed, but when they emerge they can be overwhelming. If it is true that capitalism flourishes on growth and dies on stagnation, then the market response to the environmental crisis so long ignored by its theorists may be woefully inadequate to the magnitude of the problem.

A number of revisionist market economists, reacting in part to problems internal to neoclassical theory and in part to a growing perception that the theory does not correspond to the actual economic system at crucial points, have introduced some adjustments into this framework. A recent study by A. Myrick Freeman, Robert H. Haveman, and Allen V. Kneese, *The Economics of Environmental Policy*,[10] applies such a revisionist view to an understanding of environmental issues. They seek to show how the "economics of environmental management" can enable us to curb the worst effects of pollution within the parameters of the market economy. Their basic acceptance of the market model is expressed when they assert that "unlike most other kinds of resources, choices involving the allocation of environmental resources cannot be left to individuals acting separately in unregulated and decentralized markets."[11]

But then some adjustments are made in the theory they employ. They concede that manipulative advertising affects consumer choices in important ways. They acknowledge that a highly unequal distribution of income allows privileged minorities to impose the heaviest burdens of pollution and the largest costs of pollution control on low-income groups. They agree that their proposals to incorporate ecological costs into the pricing system are inadequate to cope with costs to future generations. They agree that biases in the pluralist political system make it an exceedingly intractable vehicle for incorporating environmental costs into the market system. Indeed, they conclude, "the most formidable barrier to controlling pollution is probably not technology, population or public attitudes, but the politics of power."[12]

These adjustments could provide the catalyst for a quite different analysis of environmental issues. But these leads are not pursued by the authors. Inequality is noted as a problem, but neither its causes nor environmental effects are explored.[13] The costs for future generations are mentioned, but *institutional reforms* that might enable citizens to forgo immediate consumption benefits to preserve the future environment are never considered. Biases in the pluralist political system are described as the most "formidable barrier" to ecological integrity, but only a brief (and rather quaint) reference is made to "institutional arrangements such as the congressional seniority system and loose campaign financial regulations that encourage economic power to be readily transformed into political power."[14] In effect, these modifications function to protect specific parts of the theory while its basic form remains untouched: The newly identified factors, though admitted to be important, are neither explained within the model nor reflected in policy proposals drawn from it.

Such an analysis moves too hesitantly beyond those very assumptions that led social scientists to ignore the environmental effects of prevailing arrangements until they reached near crisis proportions. The analysis is abstracted from the basic structure of corporate capitalism. The technical proposals for reform do not show a grasp of the political constituencies and structural reforms required to implement them. In fact, proposals to incorporate environmental costs into the market system while retaining the structural arrangements that have generated these effects promise to divide the very constituencies that must be united if environmental deterioration is to be forestalled.

These are the charges we seek to sustain. To do so, we must

move beyond the artificial division between the economic and political systems postulated in the market model to a perspective that probes connections between the dangerous deterioration of the natural environment and the political economy of corporate capitalism.

Product Alternatives and Corporate Priorities

To specify the cause of a problem is to establish as well its appropriate remedy. If otherwise healthy markets fail to price the social costs of resource depletion and pollution, the solution is to build those costs artificially into market transactions. But if the *power* of corporations to impose their priorities on *governments* and *markets* is part of the problem and if some of those priorities in turn flow from structural tendencies in corporate capitalism, then the remedy will involve major reforms in the political economy. It is the latter hypothesis that we wish to defend. We will start by exploring three related areas of production and consumption: transportation, energy, and petrochemical products.

Transportation

A national transportation system built around automobiles, trucks, and airplanes uses fuel and metal resources extravagantly, imposes an enormous load on the self-purification capacities of the ecosystem, and increases the transportation costs of low-income families. Assuming each vehicle to be half full, it takes ten gallons of gasoline per person to fly from Boston to New York, seven gallons per person by car, and only two gallons per person by train.[15]

If mass transit systems were introduced into our urban areas to replace commuting by automobiles, 50 percent of the fuel now consumed by automobiles could be saved. And since it takes six times as much fuel to haul a ton of freight from Los Angeles to New York by truck as it does by rail, it is clear that the truck imposes similar strains on the fuel resources and waste absorption capacities of the environment.[16]

Why does the United States depend on such an irrational transportation system, and what stops us from shifting to more economical forms? A large part of the answer lies in the rising influence of the automobile corporations in the first part of the twentieth century.

During the 1920s the United States had rather extensive trolley, transit, and rail systems, and there was ample potential to expand these services to meet the needs of a growing industrial population.

The dissolution of these systems is not sufficiently explained through reference to a history of informed consumer choices in a competitive economy, nor is such an explanation adequate to explain the contemporary pressure against the redeployment of rail and transit systems.

As Bradford Snell has documented in a report to the Senate Judiciary Subcommittee on Antitrust and Monopoly,[17] the competitive situation of the 1920s was short-lived. During the middle of the decade General Motors, often in conjunction with Standard Oil of California and Firestone Tire, launched an investment program enabling it first to control and then to dismantle the electric trolley and transit systems of forty-four urban areas in sixteen states. Often operating through a holding company, National City Line, the three corporations acquired electric rail systems, uprooted the tracks, and substituted diesel-powered bus systems. After acquisition and conversion, the systems were sold back to local groups, but only with a contractual clause precluding the purchase of new equipment "using any fuel or means of propulsion other than gas."[18]

The life of a diesel bus is 28 percent shorter than that of its electric counterpart; its operating costs are 40 percent higher. Thus the typical result of substituting one system for the other was "higher operating costs, loss of patronage, and eventual bankruptcy."[19] General Motors pursued a similar program of acquisition and conversion with rail lines.

General Motors and its satellite companies benefited in two ways from this policy. First, its profits from the sale of buses and diesel-powered locomotives are higher than from trolleys and electric trains. Second, the financial difficulties faced by these converted transportation systems encouraged consumers to buy more cars. General Motors' *incentive* to make cars and trucks the basic vehicles of American ground transportation is clear enough: Its gross revenues are ten times greater if it sells cars rather than buses and twenty-five to thirty-five times greater if it sells trucks rather than locomotives.[20] Its expansion into mass transportation systems enhanced its ability to attract consumers to cars and trucks rather than to alternative modes of ground transportation.

The policy of acquiring, converting, selling, and strangling mass transportation systems, in combination with the escalating pressure from the American Road Builders Association, American Trucking Association, and American Petroleum Association to launch massive state and federal highway construction programs, helped to make trucks and automobiles dominant vehicles for shipping and transportation in the country.[21] Sandwiched between a private corporation with impressive market power over ground transportation and a government pressure system biased in favor of those organized corporate interests that pressed successfully for $156 billion in highway construction between 1945 and 1970, mass transportation systems inevitably lost out.

But as profitable as the operation was to the corporations involved, it was disastrous for the country. Besides the strain it imposes on our fuel resources, it has created cities criss-crossed with highways, straddled by distorted housing patterns, and smothered in toxic emissions of carbon monoxide, lead, and other deadly chemical combinations from gasoline-powered vehicles.

It is absurd to argue that consumers have chosen cars and trucks over transit and rail systems after having considered each option in the light of its comparative costs and benefits, including the costs of highway construction and the effects on the environment. Rather, a few corporations with effective market power, including control over information about alternative transportation, helped to eliminate some modes of transportation as viable consumer options and thereby stimulated consumer demand for the only options left. Thereafter, market control in this area was further solidified as national patterns of employment (automobile factories, oil production, highway construction) and satellite entrepreneurial activities (motels, tourist businesses) developed around this system and established a vast constituency whose immediate interests are tied to the maintenance and expansion of an ecologically irrational transportation system.

Energy

Between October 17, 1973, and January 1, 1974, Americans became thoroughly aware of the nation's dependence on foreign energy supplies. At that time, Arab nations imposed a boycott on oil to industrial nations, restricting energy use by American consumers, and doubled the price of crude oil, sending consumer prices skyward.

The energy crunch, it is often asserted, converted the recession of the mid-1970s into a near depression, one which took the form of high inflation and high unemployment.[22] But this explanation stops where it should begin. Why has the United States become so dependent on Arab oil and thereby so vulnerable to boycotts and price increases? What do our expanding energy needs imply for the future?

As we have already seen, the American political economy cannot sustain full employment unless it achieves a rather high rate of growth. That growth in the past has been fueled by a large and cheap supply of energy, especially oil. Thus United States oil consumption increased from 2.37 to 6.4 billion barrels a year between 1950 and 1973. Between 1960 and 1972 alone, while our total energy consumption rose by 60 percent, no increase was made in our capacity to extract fuel from the earth. Instead we relied more and more on cheap fuels from abroad. If present trends continue, the dependence will deepen: "Before the Arab boycott we were importing one third of our oil supplies; if we return to a business-as-usual posture, we could well be importing one half of our oil supplies by 1980."[23]

The energy crunch of 1973 was thus anchored in our dependence on foreign oil, which in turn was rooted in the growth imperatives of corporate capitalism as well as in the wasteful patterns of consumption based on cheap and plentiful fuel supplies. Within this broad framework, more specific features deserve attention.

1. The waste in our energy supply system is unbelievable. One third of the oil discovered in any oil reservoir is actually lifted out. Fifty percent of the coal is left behind in deep coal mining. And conversion processes are equally wasteful. Only 20 percent of the energy potential of oil is employed in the automobile engine; 60 percent of energy potential is lost in the conversion of coal into electricity.[24] These figures only symbolize the immense amounts of energy lost in mining, distribution, and conversion processes.

2. Electric utilities have rates set by public authorities. But they offer the lowest rates to the biggest users, encouraging large users to substitute electricity for less wasteful forms of energy. Electric rates are also set on a cost-plus basis, discouraging managers from seeking ways to curb costs of materials and production.

3. Oil companies drill and refine oil for profit. Neither the oil industry nor any government agency is charged with ensuring that the supply of oil in the United States matches its oil needs. As things stand, oil companies can be stimulated to meet oil needs only by government incentives that make it profitable for them to expand.

4. While established energy resources are being rapidly depleted or left open to the vagaries of international politics, the United States government has concentrated its research and development of energy alternatives in one area: nuclear energy. That policy leads to reliance on a fuel with serious storage problems for the radioactive wastes it secretes and increases the likelihood that the plutonium necessary for the construction of nuclear weapons will become widely available.

5. Competition between companies controlling alternative

energy sources has declined. Coal, which was a rather competitive industry, underwent a wave of mergers during the 1960s. By 1969 the thirteen largest coal producers accounted for 51 percent of coal production. Since part of the remaining coal production is in the hands of consuming companies, such as steel, this figure understates the extent of oligopoly. More important, the most significant mergers cut across the energy industries. In 1962 the oil industry accounted for 2 percent of coal production, but by 1969 it accounted for 25 percent. The oil companies have indeed diversified effectively, for by 1969 the four largest oil firms had acquired holdings in gas, oil, shale, tar sands, and uranium.[25] Such concentration decreases interfuel price competition and enables the oil industry to influence the type and supply of energy in its favor. As David Freeman, a student of energy resources in the United States, has concluded:

> One does not have to subscribe to a conspiracy theory to observe that a shortage of energy is a situation most favorable to the energy companies. Concentration within the industry makes it less likely that any producers will scramble to enlarge supplies unless profit margins are most attractive.[26]

6. The energy industry complex, led by oil, matches its market power with impressive leverage over government officials. Its huge contributions to presidential and congressional candidates, the secret and illegal political funds held by Gulf Oil and other oil companies, its favored policy treatment including the earlier oil depletion allowance and oil import quotas, all testify to the political power of energy corporations. It would take strong leadership by the President to launch needed new programs of energy research and development into the ecologically promising areas of solar energy, geothermal power, tides, wind power, and organic wastes. But no President has been eager to take on the oil companies; to do so would be to write off immediately the electoral college votes of Texas and to unleash a well-financed campaign of vilification against him. Any President who called for nationalization of energy would risk even more militant responses. The combined market and government power of the oil companies makes it exceedingly difficult to develop alternative energy forms *until* the energy problem itself attains crisis proportions.

Petrochemicals
The chemical revolution of the post-World War II period allowed many commodities to be made of synthetic rather than organic sub-

stances. Detergents replaced soap, synthetic fibers replaced cotton and wool, plastics substituted for leather, rubber and wood, and large infusions of synthetic fertilizers for intensive land cultivation replaced the organic fertilizers tied to more extensive land use. Barry Commoner has demonstrated that such a substitution of synthetic for organic materials is almost always incompatible with ecological imperatives; for the "chemical substances . . . which are absent from biological systems are, for that reason, frequently toxic and/or non-biodegradable."[27] Typically, too, each synthetic material requires more energy for its production than does its organic counterpart.

Again, neither sovereign voters nor sovereign consumers can be said to have chosen these materials over their organic counterparts in the light of an informed assessment of the comparative utility of each option. In agriculture, once some farmers had used more synthetic fertilizers, market competition required all farmers to do so. Oligopolistic soap companies found that detergents were more profitable than soap—even though wastes from soap are far less destructive of soil and waterways. And petrochemical companies generally found the sale of synthetics to be more profitable in the short run than the sale of organic materials.

In the areas of transportation, energy production, and petrochemicals, then, product decisions with adverse environmental effects reflect the private priorities of corporations with massive market power. This market power in turn generates a work force and a set of satellite companies that depend on these corporations for employment and market outlets. Thus if environmentalists press to convert to energy resources and product forms that are better for the ecology, the dependent workers and businesses will emerge as a powerful political constituency in support of prevailing corporate policies. Truckers will oppose a shift to rail freight systems; auto and steel workers will oppose mass transit systems; tire, oil, and highway construction firms will make political payoffs to protect the status quo.

Moreover, since the multinational corporation has kept its autonomous investment and pricing prerogatives, it can arouse these dependent constituencies when government regulatory policies threaten to become effective. For example, if domestic regulations prove too stringent, the corporation can divert a portion of its capital to other countries where environmental controls are much weaker. The resulting threat of domestic unemployment will mobilize affected workers and businesses to support the corporation's domestic economic policies.

The multinational corporation's domestic and foreign market power helps to create powerful political leverage in support of its economic autonomy. The resulting combination of power over markets and government policies makes market theories of the economy and pluralist theories of politics increasingly anachronistic. A rational ecology policy requires that the private corporation, presently unaccountable to the public, be brought under full public control; and the political coalition needed to advance that policy, we will argue, can only emerge if white-collar environmentalists revise their priorities to reflect more closely the pressing needs of blue-collar workers.

The Environment and the Worker

In the political economy of corporate capitalism the work environment of the blue-collar worker is too often filled with deadly fumes, carcinogenic dust, high noise levels, and intense heat. Periodically a major mine disaster or a particularly harsh outbreak of cancer among workers handling deadly chemicals arouses public awareness and mobilizes support for reform of the work environment. But typically conditions return to normal as public attention shifts elsewhere. One earlier incident, exceptional in the death and injury produced, exposes strikingly this cycle of brief uproar and longer periods of benign neglect.

In 1930, as the depression was deepening, workers were too weak to insist on health standards, and the public was kept ignorant about the most oppressive conditions of work. A subsidiary of Union Carbide began a hydroelectric project in the southern part of West Virginia, diverting water from two rivers through a tunnel to be constructed near the town of Gauley Bridge. The Gauley Bridge disaster, as it came to be known when finally it became a public issue five years after the fact, involved a group of mostly black, unskilled workers who dug the tunnel through silica rock.

Working for extremely low pay, breathing carbon monoxide fumes as they rode into the tunnel every day, the workers also inhaled the heavy clouds of silica dust created by rock blasting in the tunnel. Engineers wore masks inside the tunnel, for the adverse effects of silica dust inhalation were even then known to health officials. But no masks were assigned to the workers. As increasing numbers of workers died from exposure to the dust, Rinehart-Dennis, the subcontractor on the project, hired a local undertaker to bury the bodies at fifty-five dollars per corpse.

When the U.S. Public Health Service probed the disaster in 1935, it concluded that 476 men had died and 1500 had been disabled. The case was eventually tried in the courts, and congressional hearings were held, but the effective legal and legislative response was negligible. The settlements for survivors were extremely small; some defense lawyers were even caught accepting bribes from the company. The congressional hearings did not result in effective health regulations. And none of the companies involved, New Kanawha Power, Rinehart-Dennis, and Union Carbide, ever faced official punitive action.[28]

Despite recent legislation designed to protect the health and safety of workers, the classic cycle persists. Consider some of the facts about work and health in America today:

The Public Health Service estimates that each year prolonged exposure to toxic chemicals, dusts, noise, heat, cold, and radiation kills 100,000 workers and disables 390,000 more.

A federally sponsored, and more intensive, study of workers in a variety of factories and farms disclosed that three out of every ten workers suffered occupationally related illnesses. Ninety percent of these illnesses were not reported through regular channels, suggesting that the Public Health estimates are seriously deflated.

While Congress was moving in 1974 to reduce Occupational Safety and Health Administration (OSHA) funds for inspection of safety and health protection of employees in small businesses, another study showed that one out of every four workers in a sample of small businesses incurred an occupationally related disease. Eighty-nine percent of these were not reported to the Labor Department. The diseases included chronic respiratory disorders, loss of hearing, eye cataracts, and increased lead absorption in the blood.[29]

Within these general statistics are particular areas of extreme suffering and neglect:

Three million workers in fabricated metals, stone, clay, and glass products suffer a very high incidence of irreversible respiratory diseases such as silicosis, byssinosis, and emphysema.

The death rate among coal miners from respiratory diseases is five times higher than that of the general population.

Asbestos workers are disproportionately afflicted with asbestiosis, which is in turn linked to cancer of the lung, stomach, colon, and rectum.

Coke workers in steel factories assigned to the ovens for five years or more incur a risk of cancer ten times greater than that of the general population.

One out of every six uranium miners will die of cancer within ten years.

Employees in petroleum-based mineral oils suffer a very high incidence of cancer. [30]

Passage of the Occupational Safety and Health Act of 1970 seemed to promise rectification of this miserable record of worker illness and death, but the effectiveness of its administrative and research arm, OSHA, has been severely limited. Of the half million synthetic substances introduced into the work environment, threshold limits had been established for only 250 by 1974. Though the agency proposed new standards for a variety of toxic substances in 1971, including inorganic lead, carbon monoxide, arsenic and sulphuric dioxide, the standards had not been enacted by time of printing. Indeed, the Nader Health Research Group contended in 1974 that Nixon campaign strategists used the promise of relaxed OSHA controls to gain large contributions from business elites during the 1972 campaign. And a memorandum published by the Senate Watergate Committee quotes a Nixon official promising that "no highly controversial standards (i.e., cotton, dust, etc.) will be proposed by OSHA" during the next four Nixon years. [31]

By 1974 OSHA was hamstrung in a variety of ways: With less than 800 inspectors in the field, the average employer will see an inspector once every sixty-six years; after three years of operation only two firms had been convicted of criminal violations; and the average fine for OSHA violations is twenty-five dollars. [32]

Clearly the work place is a major site of ecological assault, but just as clearly corporate and business elites use the impressive resources at their disposal to hide the facts about worker disease, to deflect pressures for reform of the work environment into other channels, and to malign those who would convert the oppressive conditions of work into a public issue. The U.S. Chamber of Commerce reflected this orientation when it told health officials, "The health of American industry is eroded every time a new standard is issued."[33]

Blue-collar workers have traditionally been wary of environmentalism, partly because the issues as defined by leading environmentalists have bypassed the work place. It has appeared to many workers, and often correctly so, that environmental reforms would undermine the standard of living of the working class without bringing tangible benefits in return. But if the ecology movement, currently facing hard times, were to identify the work place itself as the crucial place to promote environmentalism, the prospects for a political alliance between workers and environmentalists would be enhanced.

Work Life and Incentive Systems

Workers are victimized not only by the work place as a collection point for pollution and safety and health hazards. The structure of work itself is deadening for vast numbers of blue- and white-collar workers: The incentive system that structure sustains and the motivational system it accentuates produce exactly the set of consumer pressures that must be displaced if environmental degradation is to be forestalled.

Routinized, repetitive, mindless work that only imperfectly produces goods and services for the general welfare cannot be intrinsically satisfying to the workers. In such circumstances, work must be organized almost completely around external incentives. Since continuous interclass and intergeneration movement in a highly stratified society officially committed to class mobility ("equality of opportunity") erodes extended kinship ties and breaks up stable neighborhood communities, the external incentives to work must be restricted to a narrow range. Incentives tied to the general welfare of internally unified collectivities (for instance, community recreation centers, health programs, transit systems) tend to be displaced by incentives tied to private consumer goods (like stylish clothes, exotic foods) or to goods that can be enjoyed by the individual primarily within the nuclear family (for instance, cars, television sets, private houses).

We do not say, of course, that all consumer satisfactions geared to private individuals and to nuclear families are evil; nor do we think that a work incentive system tied strictly to collective goals would be feasible or desirable. But it is clear that private incentives are unnecessarily accentuated by the structure of work and social life that prevails in our society, while the connection between fulfilling work and the attainment of more durable, collective interests is ignored. Deprived of the opportunity for communal satisfaction in and out of work, workers seek their satisfactions privately. This limited range of private satisfactions must then become the main incentive to work and the main form of consumption.

The organization of work, the restriction of opportunities for improvement to *individual* mobility, and the resulting erosion of stable communal ties combine to sustain (or to require) a private mode of life that is intrinsically unfulfilling and opposed to the imperatives of ecology. Public policies that seek to change patterns of *consumption* to ecologically rational forms while leaving this historically specific set of *productive* and *social* arrangements untouched are doomed to magnify the discontent of those caught in the bind. Until these structural sources of consumerism are confronted, either consumerism itself will prevail or its magnitude will be reduced by forcing "sacrifices" from those who are already the most exploited.

For instance, should I voluntarily support a transit system in this area when I can improve my own life chances only by moving elsewhere in a few years? Are the costs of recycling and of modernizing waste disposal systems worth it to us when there is no internalized *we* that any of us naturally identifies with? Is the future condition of this stream, this park, this local atmosphere, this soil of deep concern to me when my relatives live elsewhere and my children are also likely to move? When I am likely to be a transitory resident myself? Will I tolerate high tax levels and the curtailment of consumer purchases to protect the environment for others when the promise of consumer pleasures and the dangers of personal insecurity provide my basic incentives to work?

Economists and other social scientists gripped by the theory of abstract individualism, by the view of individuals as private utility maximizers, are unable to explore the ecological import of these structural arrangements. They simply assume that the incentives to work must always and everywhere match those dominant in our society. They suppose the private consumer satisfactions predominant here to be the paradigm satisfaction available to the human species. In effect, they take as given what needs to be explained. When confronting the basic dimensions of work, social life, and patterns of motivation in our society, one must not lose sight of the simple insight enunciated in another context by E. E. Schattschneider:

*Anyone watching the crowds move about Grand Central Station
might learn something. . . . The crowds seem to be completely unorganized. What the spectator observes is not chaos,
however, because the multitude is controlled by the timetables
and the gates.* Each member of the crowd finds his place in the
system (is organized by the system) because his alternatives
are limited.[34]

Those who, analogously, comprehend that the prevailing patterns of work and opportunity in our stratified social order provide a
set of timetables and gates to shape and limit the modes of life open
to citizens will understand as well that efforts to channel consumption habits into ecologically sound forms will be resisted bitterly by
those confined within these structures. In the absence of new possibilities for fulfillment in work itself, in the absence of new possibilities for stable community relationships that extend beyond the
nuclear family, apprehensive blue- and white-collar workers will
militantly oppose environmental management programs that
threaten the private forms of satisfaction currently available. The
organizations to which they belong can be expected to coalesce with
corporate interests to oppose environmental controls.

There is nothing about the environmental crisis itself that ensures the political will and muscle to correct it. The pressures
against environmentalism are indeed very strong. But an environmental movement that connects prevailing structures of work and
opportunity with persisting patterns of environmental destruction
has the best potential to build a progressive coalition that could
correct the one form of exploitation while coping with the other.

Inequality and Social Services

We have already considered arguments for, and barriers to, a reduction of economic inequality. It remains to add that ecology and
equality are closely connected; progress in one area can contribute
to success in the other.

The basic relation, enunciated in a different context by Jean
Jacques Rousseau, is quite simple and powerful. In a highly stratified, individualistic society those with the most wealth and income
seek private solutions to collective problems, often deepening the
collective problems as they escape them individually. Those in the
lowest positions, however, lack both the means to secure private
remedies to these troubles and the power to impose public solutions.

In an egalitarian society, by contrast, it is rational for each citizen to support public solutions to those collective problems that none is in a position to escape privately. And for such a disposition in favor of the public interest to prevail, it is not necessary that absolute equality be established: "As for equality, this word must not be understood to mean that all individuals must have exactly the same amount of power and wealth, but rather that power must be exercised . . . so that no one shall have so much of it as to be able to do violence upon another and that no citizen shall have so much wealth that he can buy another, and none so little that he is forced to sell himself."[35]

In the American class system the affluent evade urban pollution, congestion, noise, and heat by private expenditures that at once accelerate environmentally destructive practices and undermine the political will of privileged minorities to cope with these public consequences. The affluent can secure work that is environmentally safe, move to suburbs where the air and water are cleaner, live in large, private homes, escape summer heat through air conditioning, take vacations by jet to undefiled areas, locate residences away from nuclear plants, replace shoddy products that break or perish. Indeed, in the absence of *public* policies to attack the pertinent environmental problems, it is rational for the affluent to use private resources to fund such *private* escapes. But since they must then commute to work in the inner city by automobile, their private escape worsens the pollution problem in the city they left behind. Their dependence on air conditioning, wasteful heating systems, air travel, and shoddy products similarly increases the load imposed on the environment. Most important, since they have invested heavily in private escape and since their own affluence often flows from ecologically unsound business enterprises, they tend then to oppose public policies that would make energy production ecologically safe, establish mass transit systems, improve building construction codes to reduce the energy wasted in heating and air conditioning, restore urban parks and waterways, improve urban garbage and disposal systems, ensure the production of more durable goods, encourage the shift from synthetic to organic materials in consumer goods, and so on. The very availability of expensive private escape routes makes the affluent unwilling to accept the tax assessments, changes in production processes, and alterations in privileged life styles necessary to apply collective solutions to these public problems.

In these interconnected ways, inequality combines with the system of corporate priorities, the structure of work, and the weakness of communal ties to encourage the growth of ecologically devastating forms of consumption. It imposes the most direct and oppressive effects of these unsound systems on a politically weak underclass. Inequality encourages the affluent to seek private escape routes that deepen the system's debt to nature. And it dampens political support for effective public programs. These are the reasons that redistribution, a worthy objective in its own right, will also form an essential part of any political movement that seriously hopes to cope with the environmental crisis. These considerations also reinforce the case for bringing the private corporation under effective public control, for inequality cannot be materially reduced until corporate pricing, investment, salary, and location decisions are subjected to public debate and accountability.

A more egalitarian society would not *necessarily* maintain rational ecological policies, but it would be *more likely* to do so. For, to paraphrase Rousseau, when life chances are distributed so that all can feel the effects of collective achievements and collective failures, so that all are in a position to benefit from a public resolution of common problems, and so that none can afford to escape the problems through the use of private resources unavailable to others, then the political system is very likely to generate collective responses to the common risks and burdens imposed by the depletion of nonrenewable energy resources and the deterioration of air, water, and soil supports essential to human life.

Environmental Imperatives and Political Realism

When the market model of environmental management is stripped of its theoretical props, its advocates still retain a fall-back position. The alternative model, they say, is unrealistic politically (it is naive, utopian, impractical). At least the program of "internalizing the externalities" within existing market mechanisms has a chance of gaining political acceptance. We agree. But a few additional points are required to fill this picture out.

1. If the market program is now to be justified not because it copes effectively with imperfections in an otherwise healthy system, but because theoretically viable alternatives are unacceptable to corporate and government elites, the argument for political realism becomes an indictment of the American political economy rather than a justification of the market system.

2. Neoclassical economists and pluralist political scientists who have helped to legitimize the market images of the economy and the polity bear a measure of responsibility for the political unrealism of

efforts to institute structural reforms today. Scholars who now see defects in assumptions underlying these models, and who define themselves as defenders of the truth, are today obligated to explore the theoretical viability of alternative responses to environmental control, even if these alternatives presently face intractable political barriers.

3. The policies of the environmental managers may gain limited short-run support, especially from constituencies who can easily assimilate the costs involved or displace them to subordinate classes. But initial successes, as the "war on poverty" demonstrated, can contribute to defeat over the longer run. The program of the environmental managers, as we have argued, promises to drive that segment of labor employed in the corporate sector into an alliance with corporate elites against environmental reform. The immediate difficulties in our strategy are outstripped only by the long-run political unrealism of the economics of environmental management. Moreover, labor-corporate backlash threatens to heighten the repressive tendencies in American politics.

4. When one construes the problem as political rather than technical, it is clear that the most important strategic objective is to mobilize a progressive labor-environmentalist coalition around issues immediately compelling to each and thus to generate momentum for more basic reforms at a later date. Such a strategy is not easy to develop. But the most promising focal point is the work place itself. Workers and environmentalists can find common ground in an effort to eliminate the hazards of pollution within the work place. And as environmentalists come to see that the reform of work life is an essential precondition to sound environmental control, that alliance could develop into a movement for broader structural reform.

Clearly, the direction the environmental movement takes in the next few years will help to determine whether a labor-environmental or labor-corporate coalition gains ascendancy. If economic growth no longer matches the pace of the 1960s (as we expect) and if the organized labor movement does coalesce with corporate elites, we can expect a suppression of environmental issues while labor in the corporate sector solidifies its advantages over labor in the market sector of the economy. If, alternatively, an emerging alliance between environmentalists and organized labor forestalls these developments, there is a chance that the "economics of environmental management" can be replaced by the politics of work-life reform, income redistribution, and environmental integrity.

No one group can alone shape forces as large as those discussed here, but a strategically alert environmental movement can encourage the labor-environmentalist coalition necessary to attack the institutional sources of environmental decay.

NOTES

1. In Paul Samuelson's classic text, *Economics* (New York: McGraw-Hill, 1948, 1951, 1955, 1958, 1961, 1964, 1967, 1970, 1973) there is no discussion of pollution until the 1961 edition, where a very brief mention of smoke is made. By 1964 there were a couple of paragraphs on "external diseconomies" in general; by 1967 a brief justification of government intervention to compensate for market externalities such as air and water pollution. There is no comparable classic text in political science. But Frederic Ogg and R. Orman Ray, *Essentials of American Government* (New York: Appleton-Century-Crofts, 1932, 1936, 1940, 1943, 1947, 1950, 1952, 1961, 1963, 1969), covers a long span and has been widely used. The 1950 edition contains a brief, optimistic discussion of recent government protection of land, soil, water, forest, and mineral resources. By 1969, William and Sara Young, who revised that edition, warned that "our forests are still being slashed and depleted; soil is being washed and blown away. . . . Bays and estuaries, rivers and lakes are brown with silt and rank with wastes. Our cities are choked with traffic, smog and blight" (p. 400). A more contemporary, behavioral text, Marian D. Irish and James W. Prothro, *The Politics of American Democracy* (Englewood Cliffs, N.J.: Prentice Hall, 1959, 1962, 1965, 1968), has four chapters dealing with the "outputs of the political system," but none touch the politics of ecology.
2. K. W. Kapp, *The Social Costs of Private Enterprise* (Cambridge, Mass.: Harvard University Press, 1950); Grant McConnell, "The Conservation Movement: Past and Present," *Western Political Quarterly* (December 1954), pp. 463–478, and *Private Power and American Democracy* (New York: Knopf, 1966).
3. Kapp, p. 229.
4. Ibid., pp. 229, 230.
5. Ibid., p. 236.
6. McConnell, *Private Power and American Democracy*, pp. 129, 247.
7. This analysis is developed in Garret Hardin, "The Tragedy of the Commons," *Science* (December 13, 1968), pp. 1243–1248, and Kenneth Arrow, "The Organization of Economic Activity: Issues Pertinent to the Choice of Market Versus Non-Market Allocation," in *Public Expenditures and Public Analysis*, ed. Robert Haveman and Jerrold Margolis (Chicago: Markham, 1970).

8. There are other difficulties more or less internal to this theory that we cannot discuss here: the assumption of a smooth exchange function between any two items (how many ice cream cones will you exchange for your left arm?); the assumption that the environment (including animals) is merely to be viewed and valued as a human resource; and (a view we will oppose in our alternative model) the tendency to reduce complex social relationships to exchange relationships between private utility maximizers. For impressive elaboration and criticism of these tendencies among utilitarians in general and market economists in particular, see Stuart Hampshire, *Morality and Pessimism* (London: Cambridge University Press, 1973); Robert Paul Wolff, *The Poverty of Liberalism* (Boston: Beacon Press, 1968), ch. 5, and Lawrence Tribe, "The Policy Sciences: Science or Ideology?" *Philosophy and Public Affairs* (Fall 1972), pp. 66–110.

9. See Robert Heilbroner, "The Human Prospect," *New York Review of Books*, January 4, 1974), pp. 21–34.

10. (New York: Wiley, 1973).

11. Ibid., p. 33.

12. Ibid., p. 170.

13. As the authors put it, "We must assume that there is some political mechanism through which collective choices are made and that through this political mechanism the society has determined the rules that govern the distribution of income and wealth in the society." Ibid., p. 70.

14. Ibid., p. 168.

15. S. David Freeman, *Energy: The New Era* (New York: Vintage Books, 1974), p. 128.

16. Barry Commoner, *The Closing Circle* (New York: Knopf, 1971), p. 169.

17. Bradford Snell, *American Ground Transport: A Proposal for Reconstructing the Automobile, Truck, Bus, and Rail Industries*, presented to the Subcommittee on Antitrust and Monopoly of the Committee of the Judiciary, U. S. Senate (Washington: Government Printing Office).

18. Ibid., p. 37.

19. Ibid.

20. Ibid., p. 38. General Motors did, according to findings by the Interstate Commerce Commission, make cost claims for its diesel locomotives to potential buyers that were "erroneous," "inflated," and "manifestly absurd" (Ibid., p. 41), and corporate elites knew about the dangerous levels of pollution from cars and trucks as early as 1953. Nevertheless our argument leans less on an assessment of corporate intent formed in the 1920s to dismantle trolley and train systems than on the identification of *policy tendencies* that emerge when a small group of corporations dominate all forms of ground transportation, some of which are more profitable than others.

Moreover, as this brief review indicates, the acknowledgement by Freeman, Haveman, and Kneese that consumer "tastes and preferences are not strictly given, but are subject to the influences of advertising" barely scratches the surface of the forces at work in corporate capitalism that shape consumer demand by controlling product options (*The Economics of Environmental Policy*, p. 71).

21. A good summary of this development is found in Lawrence Kohlmeier, *The Regulators* (New York: Harper and Row, 1969). Notable in the history of this development was the presidential commission in 1944 that proposed the Highway Trust Fund in which gasoline taxes are used only for highway construction. The Commission "failed to give any consideration to the relative efficiency or need of rail, water and air, as well as highway transportation" (p. 154).

22. See, for example, the *New York Times* editorial, September 22, 1974.

23. Freeman, *Energy*, p. 119.

24. Ibid., pp. 201–202. See also Geoffrey Barraclough, "The Great World Crisis," *New York Review of Books* (January 1975), pp. 20–29.

25. Freeman, pp. 154–155.

26. Ibid., p. 155.

27. Commoner, p. 41.

28. A more thorough discussion of this incident, and many others as well, can be found in Joseph A. Page and Mary Win O'Brien, *Bitter Wages* (New York: Grossman, 1973), ch. 3.

29. Information for the above items is taken from the *New York Times*, March 4, 1974, May 12, 1975, and April 28, 1975.

30. These estimates, and others, are found in Frederick Wallick, *The American Worker: An Endangered Species* (New York: Ballantine, 1972); Jean Stellman and Susan Daum, *Work Is Dangerous to Your Health* (New York: Vintage, 1973); *Work in America*, Special Task Force Report to the Department of Health, Education and Welfare (Cambridge, Mass.: M.I.T. Press, 1973).

31. David Burnham, "Nader Group Says Labor Department Lagged on Health Rules to Spur Gifts," *New York Times*, July 16, 1974. The same memo emphasizes "the great potential of OSHA as a sales point for fund raising."

32. *Wall Street Journal*, August 9, 1974.

33. Ibid.

34. *The Semi-Sovereign People* (New York: Holt, Rinehart and Winston 1960), p. 57.

35. *The Social Contract* (Chicago: Regnery, 1954), p. 76.

The Politics
of Work

The Myth of the Happy Worker Explodes

Employers in the United States have traditionally taken an instrumental view of the work their employees do: The employer seeks to make a profit from production, and the employee's incentive to work efficiently is the promise of pay or the threat of unemployment.[1] With notable exceptions, most American social scientists have taken this instrumental work ethic for granted in their studies of economic processes, social relationships, and political issues.

For a long time it seemed that workers themselves shared this view. If wages, job security, and fringe benefits could be improved, it appeared that workers would remain contented with their lot. Thus, for years, between 80 and 90 percent of all polled workers responded affirmatively to the Gallup Poll question, "Is your work satisfying?"[2] And sociologist John Goldthorpe, in a detailed study of auto workers at a Vauxhall auto plant in England, found that most workers want their unions to "limit themselves to their specifically economic functions: only among the craftsmen was the idea of greater worker's control still largely upheld as a union objective."[3]

Robert Lane, a political scientist, thought he was able to explain why, despite evidence to the contrary, a small group of dissident social scientists led by Erich Fromm and C. Wright Mills, continued to speak in the 1950s of the "increasing alienation of men from work, society, and government."[4] These social scientists, Lane concluded, must be projecting their own discontents onto a contented society:

> I have long suspected that they reflect their own discontent with society rather than any mass discontent. . . . Partly, too, I think their views reflect their own alienation from the field of endeavour where there is true élan, the field of science.[5]

But then some interesting things began to happen, which cast grave doubt upon prevailing methods of survey analysis, the findings it had produced with respect to workers, and the judgments Lane and others had made about the contrary findings (and skills) of dissident social scientists.

At the Vauxhall factory, for instance, where Goldthorpe had interviewed a number of contented workers, the workers themselves began to discuss the interviews and to reconsider the statements they had made to Goldthorpe. Many agreed that they had been *individually resigned* to their jobs, but few were really *contented* with their work. And when they began to discuss their *collective* situation comparatively—as members of a working class comparing their collective plight to that of employees in other occupations—their collective sense of discontent increased. Just as Goldthorpe's findings about the lack of class consciousness were going to press, the workers struck over a local grievance that might not have otherwise have aroused them. The London *Times* report captures their response:

> Wild rioting has broken out at the Vauxhall car factories in Luton. Thousands of workers streamed out of the shops and gathered in the factory yard. They besieged the management offices, calling for the managers to come out, seizing the "Red Flag" and shouting "string them up."[6]

Indeed this sequence has been repeated on several occasions. First social scientists interview workers individually, finding them to be relatively contented, and then the factory shortly thereafter erupts unexpectedly.[7] We will later have to ask why such interview techniques tend first to miss latent resentments among those interviewed and then to encourage the very eruptions the interviewers had thought so unlikely.

Evidence of worker discontent and resentment simmering beneath verbal expressions of contentment has flourished in recent history. In France, prior to 1968, many commentators had noted the quiescence of the working force; workers were, it was popularly thought, a relatively contented lot. But in May 1968 a demonstration of students was soon transformed into a general strike of workers against the state and the capitalist system. The country was brought to a standstill.

Two characteristics marked this strike off from earlier ones. First, a new generation of young skilled workers, technicians, and white-collar workers assumed active leadership roles in this rebellion; many were recent university graduates who were supposed to be the future elite of French life. Second, the aims of the strike were nontraditional in many respects. The strikers demanded changes in the organization of worklife and the system of managerial power over workers; they demanded employee participation in decisions, greater information on company activities, better training programs.[8] The general strike finally ended when President de Gaulle pledged to institute work reforms—a promise that has yet to be delivered.

Undeniable evidence of deep worker discontent has also surfaced in the United States. The General Motors plant in Lordstown, Ohio, is its leading symbol. The Lordstown complex was designed to be a GM showpiece: New production technologies and quality controls were applied, costs were cut, worker efficiency was enhanced, high wage levels were introduced, and most important according to a GM spokesman in 1970, "the higher level of enthusiasm among employees at the Lordstown plant is producing craftsmanship to challenge any auto makers in the world."[9]

But by 1972 this enthusiasm had been replaced by increased worker absenteeism, slowdowns, sabotage, and car defects and by management's introduction of speedups, harsh disciplinary tactics, and close job monitoring. The labor-management struggles erupted finally into a bitter twenty-two-day strike. Though the strikers were eventually defeated, by the time it was over these highly paid employees with highly regimented jobs had exploded the American myth of the happy worker.

If anyone continued to have doubts, further rumblings soon removed them. Discontent was expressed by secretaries herded together into secretarial pools, young lawyers tied to routine dead-end jobs, even young middle-level managers who, according to the American Management Association, often experience "a decreasing sense of personal reward and achievement" from the "highly bureaucratic, authoritarian structure" of today's corporation.[10]

When the HEW Report *Work in America* appeared in 1973, the available evidence overwhelmingly pointed in one direction. The report summarized studies connecting low status, little autonomy, isolation, and repetitiousness of the job to the low self-esteem, anxiety, tension, passivity, and social alienation of the worker. While inequalities in income and educational levels attached to various jobs play a role in these correlations, the design of work and the structure of power in the work place are crucial factors as well.[11] And by the time it was widely publicized that only 24 percent of blue-collar and 43 percent of white-collar workers would choose the same job again if they had a chance, the problem of worker alienation had become a serious concern to those very managers and social scientists who had previously denied its existence, even though most of them translated the issue of alienation into a problem of worker "motivation."[12]

The myth of the happy worker had been dissipated by the early 1970s, but why had so many mainstream social scientists believed in that myth until *after* the worker unrest of the late 1960s and 1970s? One flimsy answer is that the workers were happy before, say, 1968, but not after. Such an answer, though, would cast doubt on the ability of survey analysts to predict future events and would hardly explain the persistence of the same working conditions and evidence of worker depression, and so on, before and after that date. A more promising course is to probe defects in the survey methods that produced the faulty findings. Such interviewing methods encourage answers that reflect the prevailing ideology of the day more than they test the actual congruence between that ideology and the life conditions of those interviewed. If the instrumental view of work is in ideological ascendancy, surveys of workers during periods of labor quiescence are likely to mesh with that ideology.[13]

When a worker is asked, "Are you satisfied with your work?", he tends to reply with the socially established model of work in mind. He says to himself, "I'm about as satisfied as one is supposed to be with work," and then answers, "yes." Moreover, when interviewed alone, he tends to *compare* himself with other workers in his job category. He is, generally, about as satisfied as they are; so again he is prone to answer yes. Finally, in the absence of available examples or theories of work that challenge the dominant work ethic and work system, the worker has no alternative conception against which to appraise his condition. Even a slave would say he is happy if his experience were so constricted that he believed slavery to be a natural and necessary condition for people like him. The worker's experience is not so thoroughly limited, but in modern capitalist society his experience with *alternative forms of work* has been severely restricted.

It is understandable, then, that workers who express satisfaction individually to interviewers have often changed their minds through collective discussion. For then *the terms of comparison* within which they are thinking and acting change. They begin to think more about their collective plight. The reaction to the interview itself encourages a shift in the terms of comparison. And, it must be remembered, statements about happiness, satisfaction, and contentment are always made within some framework of comparison, most often, given prevailing survey techniques, within the framework sustained by the dominant ideology of the society.

But to insist, as we have, that the terms of comparison one adopts are crucial in appraising a system of work is to raise a whole host of new issues: Against what standards should one appraise the system of work that prevails in our society? What are the strengths and weaknesses of the instrumental model of work when compared to this standard? If its defects are grave, why has it retained for so long its dominant position in our society?

We will approach these questions by comparing two opposed models of work. The first one, we think, views work and workers primarily with the needs of owners and employers in mind; the second speaks more fully to the needs of workers themselves. The conflict between these two models plays a profound role in the politics of our society—in the class struggle between workers and owners—even though its influence is often hidden beneath a set of more acceptable, surrogate issues that dominate public attention.

Two Models of Work

Taylorism

Frederick W. Taylor, chief engineer for a steel company in the 1880s, founded the modern principles of scientific management. He was convinced that workers in a variety of occupations could be made more productive if management would follow rigorously a set of principles he had devised and tested in the field.

His experiment with an immigrant pig-iron handler earned him a good deal of acclaim and notoriety. Each "pig" weighed 92 pounds and the handler had to pick it up and carry it a few yards to a pile. The average handler hauled $12\frac{1}{2}$ tons per day. But Taylor, by carefully selecting a hauler of low intelligence and great strength, by rearranging meticulously the method and timing of the work, and by paying the handler a bonus for following his instructions to the letter and fulfilling his quota was able to increase that output fourfold. Taylor himself describes the monitoring process:

> Schmidt started to work, and all day long, and at regular intervals, was told by the man who stood over him with a watch, "Now pick up a pig and walk. Now sit down and rest. Now work—Now rest," etc. He worked when he was told to work and rested when he was told to rest, and half past five in the afternoon had his $47\frac{1}{2}$ tons loaded on the car. . . . One man after another was picked out and trained to handle pig iron at the rate of $47\frac{1}{2}$ tons per day until all the pig iron was handled at this rate and the men were receiving 60 percent more wages than the workmen around them.[14]

With the completion and publication of this experiment the science of management was launched.

There are certain things taken for granted in Taylor's science. First, he takes as given the capitalist system of private ownership, production for profit, and wage labor. Second, his science is not a neutral science, or a science for just anyone, but a science for managers who seek to organize work so as to maximize profits and to exercise control over workers. Though Taylor insists that an effective system of work will promote "intimate, friendly cooperation between the management and the men,"[15] he also insists that a precondition for such cooperation is that the workers accept the full authority of the managers over all aspects of the production process.

The science embodies several key components.

1. Management must master and monopolize all the knowledge needed to produce a given product efficiently. The size and responsibilities of the managerial core are thus magnified under Taylor's system:

> The managers assume new burdens, new duties and responsibilities never dreamed of in the past . . . for instance, the burden of gathering together all of the traditional knowledge

which in the past has been possessed by the workmen and then of classifying, tabulating, and reducing this knowledge to rules, laws and formulae which are immensely helpful to the workers in doing their daily work.[16]

2. Management divides the production process into a series of simple components or tasks so that each task can be repeated by the same worker throughout the day. Each task is then studied intensively until the single most efficient way of doing it is discovered. This "one best method and best implement can only be discovered or developed through a scientific study and analysis of all methods and implements in use, together with accurate, minute time-and-motion study."[17]

3. Workers are selected who have the intelligence and skills needed for each particular task. Taylor thinks that most tasks should be very simple because most workers are quite simple and because the rapid repetition of simple tasks is more productive than the slower performance of complex tasks. Moreover, the "science which underlies each act of each worker is so great and amounts to so much that the workman who is best suited to actually doing the work is incapable of fully understanding the science . . . either through lack of education or through insufficient mental capacity."[18]

4. After studying the process, dividing it into a series of simple tasks, and preparing a time-and-motion study of each task, management gives each worker an assignment fitted to his abilities and then specifies precisely how he is to perform it.

The work of every workman is fully planned out by the management at least one day in advance, and each man receives in most cases complete written instructions. . . . This task specifies not only what is to be done but how it is to be done and the exact time allowed for doing it.[19]

In short, the objective is to have management do all the *mind* work while the workers do the *physical, mindless* work.

5. Each worker who performs the assignment successfully is to be paid better than those who work under different systems or who do not perform well under this system. The worker's only incentive to work is for the promise of higher pay; "personal ambition always has been and will remain a more powerful incentive to exertion than a desire for the general welfare."[20] Taylor's system of instrumental work and graded pay scales requires the very hierarchy of incomes

that the theory of functionalism (as we have seen) assumes to be necessary in every industrial society. For to maintain this system of work we must have *gradations* of pay within the work force and a significant difference in the pay between those who manage and those who are managed. Taylorism and extreme inequality therefore encourage each other: An industrial system that emphasizes either will tend to support the other as well.

Taylor demonstrated how his system of management greatly improved the productivity of pig handlers, bricklayers, shovelers, inspectors of ball bearings, and steel cutters, but he claimed that the principles could and should be applied to any productive task whatsoever: This science of management is applicable to all systems of work. And he denied the charge, already made by his critics at the turn of the century, that his system would turn workers into "wooden men." Workers might complain, he conceded, when first encountering his system, but they would soon adjust to it; they would particularly come to appreciate the increase in income it allowed. It is better, he claimed, to be a trained specialist in one area than to try, as the old frontiersman had, to be "an architect, housebuilder, lumberman, farmer, soldier and doctor" all at once. One "would hardly say," Taylor argued while carefully picking his example, that the "life of the modern surgeon is any more narrowing, or that he is more of a wooden man than the frontiersman."[21] Besides, "all of us are grown up children," and each "will work to the greatest satisfaction of both himself and his employer, when he is given each day a definite task, which constitutes a proper day's work for a good workman."[22] When managers are willing to organize work properly and to pay workers fairly for a fair day's work, and when workers come to understand that their interests harmonize with those of an enlightened management, workers, managers and the general public will all benefit. Peaceful labor-management relations will flourish in a production system that improves the prosperity of all citizens. All this, according to Taylor.

While Taylorism has acquired a bad name among many students of management and administration, its basic principles are accepted even by many who criticize this or that detail. The separation between management and workers, the assignment of mind work like planning and managing to the former and of mindless work to the latter, the division of work assignments into simple and repetitive tasks, the dependence on monetary incentives and the threat of unemployment as primary instruments of worker discipline and motivation, the use of time-and-motion studies and programmed budgets to organize work efficiently—these are still the central ingredients of modern management theory and practice. The "human relations" approach emphasized by some managerial theorists today does not undermine these basic principles in any essential way; rather it aims at surrounding the established system of work with a physical and human environment that makes it more bearable for the workers. Indeed, the human relations theorists are not as far from Taylor even in that respect as they sometimes say they are, for he, too, emphasized the need for friendly relations between workers and managers. Taylor wanted managers to be friendly and considerate while maintaining their managerial prerogatives and while managing the work others did.

Nor have political scientists or economists, save for some dissenters, subjected Taylor's principles to searching criticism. Usually these principles are taken for granted as the *natural, undebatable background* against which economic activities are studied and political issues investigated. They are thought to be outside of economics and separate from politics. Political scientists have failed to ask, for instance, why the Taylorist system of work did not become a public issue earlier in American history. It became an issue for them only after it became an issue for the public. And economists have generally adopted the principle of comparative advantage in their research: They have assumed that of two agents, if A can do one task more efficiently and B can do another more efficiently, it is rational to divide work so that A does only the first task and B only the second. A professor, for example, who can both type and write scholarly essays should never do the former if there are secretaries who write essays less effectively and type more efficiently. The secretary should only and always type while the professor should always write. Such a principle, and the minute division of labor it implies when consistently pursued, is unproblematic only to those who never consider the possible adverse effects on the people whose working lives are dominated by one activity that they repeat over and over. The principle, that is, presents no problems only to those who tacitly accept Taylor's theory of managerial control, divided work, and worker incentives.

Some critics challenged the Taylorist model of work even before it was formalized into a complete theory. Alexis de Tocqueville, for instance, studying the emerging manufacturing enterprises in the United States during the first third of the nineteenth century, was appalled by the effects this new system of work had on workers:

> *When a workman is increasingly and exclusively engaged in the fabrication of one thing, he ultimately does his work with*

singular dexterity; but at the same time, he loses the general faculty of applying his mind to the direction of his work. He everyday becomes more adroit and less industrious. In proportion as the principle of the division of labor is more extensively applied the workman becomes more weak, more narrow minded, and more dependent. The art advances, the artisan recedes. [23]

The Marxian Model of Work

Karl Marx's early writings, especially the *Economic and Philosophical Manuscripts*, set forth an alternative model of work and workers. [24] The human being, says Marx, is a "species being": "Conscious life activity distinguishes man from the life activity of animals . . . ; he is only a self-conscious being, i.e., his life is an object for him, because he is a species being." [25] It is within the capacity of human beings to appraise critically their past conduct and to revise their future activity on the basis of that appraisal. We are also able to enter into fulfilling social relationships with others, relationships that involve mutual respect and promote shared ends. Since we can appraise our common history, since we can create new projects on the basis of those appraisals, we are beings capable of self-conscious action. The capacity for self-consciousness is in fact the species character of human beings; it is what distinguishes us essentially from other forms of life.

Work, organized properly, is the most important medium through which our species life, our potential as a species, unfolds. Work is the core of our "life activity." When it is "free, conscious activity" it fulfills us. When it exercises the mind and the body together, when it involves us in cooperative endeavors with others, when we can see the results of our work projects, and when the work serves a valuable social purpose, it becomes a medium for our development and gratification. Fulfilling work cannot "be made merely a joke or amusement. . . . Really free labor, the composing of music for example, is at the same time damned serious and demands the greatest effort." [26] It is the *structure* and *purpose* of work and the *social relations* within which it is embedded that are important for Marx, not simply the difficulty or ease with which it is done.

In modern capitalist society, labor increasingly alienates workers, separates them from their species life. First, the work is undertaken out of material necessity alone; workers do it "only as *means* for satisfaction of a need, the need to maintain physical existence." [27] Work becomes instrumental only rather than becoming also a source of fulfillment in itself. Second, since work assignments are so narrowly defined the workers cannot see the individual results of the labor performed; their life activity is not ratified through viewing the product of their own craftsmanship. Third, the products a worker helps to produce are made more in the interest of making a profit for the owner than serving community welfare. The worker seldom takes pride in the social purpose served by the labor sold to another. Fourth, the fruits of labor go more to the owner and less to the worker; one works, under compulsion, not for oneself, but for another who reaps the greatest rewards from others' efforts. Fifth, and very important, the *productive process* itself is controlled not by workers but by owners; and the owners organize the process so that each worker's task is tedious and routinized. Labor neither exercises the mind nor involves cooperative relationships with other workers. It is mindless work controlled and organized by another for the other's profit.

The system of production alienates the worker, then, from the product, from creative activity, and from fellow workers—in short, from the species life:

> *The more the worker produces the less he has to consume; the more value he creates the more worthless he becomes; the more refined his product the more crude and misshapen the worker; the more civilized the product the more barbarous the worker; the more powerful the work the more feeble the worker; the more the work manifests intelligence the more the worker declines in intelligence and becomes a slave of nature.*[28]

Work in capitalist society is profoundly alienating, then, and the key to that alienation is the division of labor. It is important to see that Marx does not criticize specialization per se, although in one famous phrase (later retracted) he does celebrate the life in which one freely and frequently switches from one task to another. Rather, the "division of labor becomes truly such [is truly alienating] from the moment when a division of material and mental labor appears."[29] Such a division of labor forces some to work without thinking while it encourages others to think primarily about how to control workers. This division between mind work and mindless work is indeed a central ingredient in the class system of capitalist society.

We can see now that the models of work presented by Taylor and Marx are profoundly opposed. What seems to Taylor a rational system of ownership and division of mental and physical labor is seen by Marx as an alienating, exploitative system. The system of work that reflects human nature for Taylor treats human beings as wooden men and women, in the view of Marx. Indeed, Marx would contend that Taylor's ostensible science of management is actually a managerial ideology that falsely legitimates capital's control of worker for its own ends. Each new class in power, Marx says, "is compelled in order to carry through its aim, to represent its interest as the common interest of all members of society, put in ideal form; it will give its ideas the form of universality, and represent them as the only rational, universally valid ones,"[30] and Taylorism is the ideal form that owners and managers give to the alienating system of work they maintain in our society.

Marx would see Taylor as an ideologist whose doubtless honest beliefs serve the class interests of owners and legitimize an alienating system of work. But Taylor would think that Marxian theory is based on a faulty view of human nature and on a misunderstanding of the principles of modern production that create prosperity for all; to move away from the Taylor system would be to reduce worker productivity and to court disaster.

How is one to judge between these opposing models of work? We cannot here give that question the detailed treatment it deserves in its own right.[31] But one recent "historical experiment" does, in our view, help to shed some light on the problem.

When General Motors created the Lordstown complex it applied Taylorist principles closely in order to maximize productivity. The management assumed complete control of the organization of work; jobs were defined very narrowly; time-and-motion studies were performed to make each worker's pace and motions more efficient; workers were paid at a higher rate than the average worker receives for similar jobs. Yet the experiment failed. Only the threat of unemployment kept workers on the job. The alienating conditions themselves both damaged the workers and contributed to the sabotage, absenteeism, and relaxation of quality controls management had sought to curtail. Workers were treated like wooden men and women, and so they treated the system and product with similar contempt. This occurred, we suggest, because Taylorism is at odds with basic human needs. Taylorism can never be a source of worker fulfillment. It requires wooden men and women, and if they are not already sufficiently pliable when hired, it tries to shape them into lumber.

We do not, of course, suggest that any industrial society can altogether dispense with monetary incentives or make every job equally challenging or eliminate all routine. But a mass of evidence does suggest that work can be organized more rationally, that the disjuncture between the managers and the managed, between the mind workers and the mindless workers, can be changed, that such production processes often even enhance productivity, and that workers in such arrangements are more fulfilled and more concerned about the quality of the product or service performed.[32] Under such conditions work is not merely instrumental, something done only for pay; but it is done partly for pay, partly because of the intrinsic interest of the work, partly because of a desire to create socially useful products, and partly because of a desire to gain the respect of others through the social contribution one makes. Such a mix of incentives shows that Taylor's false dichotomy between work for private gain and work for the general welfare loads the dice in the direction of his alienating model of work: The dichotomy itself unnecessarily undermines efforts to create modes of work geared to the needs of workers as human beings.

We will assume in what follows that the model of work and the theory of human nature developed by Marx is, if sometimes overstated, on the right track. To state our position schematically (and with the absence of qualification such schematism implies), Taylorism subordinates workers to the private interest of employers in the name of productivity and prosperity for all, while unalienating work subordinates the production process to the human needs of workers in the interests of productivity and the common welfare. If Taylorism was required at one stage of industrial development (we are not sure that it was), it is no longer a necessity today in most areas of the economy.

The Expansion of Taylorism

It is useful to see the politics of work as a struggle, often indirect and sublimated, sometimes more direct and public, between workers and owners in various occupations, each group trying to institute or maintain a different model of work.[33] The owners and managers seek to institute Taylorist principles of work and managerial control, and the workers seek to create space within which the worst forms of alienation can be avoided or eliminated.

The indirect, sublimated forms of the struggle are often subtle. But in the work place itself, the grievances of workers do form a pattern. Thus the Survey Research Center at the University of Michigan, studying a large number of workers in various occupations, found that workers themselves ranked the following dimensions of work in order of importance:

1. Interesting work.
2. Enough help and equipment to get the job done.
3. Enough information to get the job done.
4. Enough authority to get the job done.
5. Good pay.
6. Opportunity to develop special abilities.
7. Job security.
8. Seeing the results of one's work.[34]

Now certainly this ranking will shift as economic conditions change. In periods of high unemployment and high inflation items 5 and 7 will surely move up on the list. This would not indicate that they are the only things that matter to workers but that when job security and pay are missing, everything else crumbles too. Workers, then, prize working conditions that reflect their humanity and their capacities for craftsmanship. Owners and managers, on the other hand, would seldom provide this rank order when discussing what they hope to promote for the workers they employ. The priorities of each group are at odds with those of the other.

The politics of work is most often part of a daily struggle carried on in local settings. In the shop where the workers' movements are prescribed and the assembly line or the timer's watch sets the workers' pace, workers will typically collaborate to create space for themselves. Here is the advice of an experienced drill press operator to a new worker about to face the rate setter:

> If you expect to get any kind of a price, you got to outwit that son-of-a-bitch! You got to use your noodle while you're working, and think your work out ahead as you go along! You got to add in movements you know you ain't going to make when you're running the job! Remember, if you don't screw them, they're going to screw you! . . . Every movement counts.[35]

Work in the factory embodies a recurring struggle between workers and managers. Management will define tasks, speed up jobs, impose new incentive systems in the interests of profit and control; workers will respond with shortcuts, group schemes, machinery breakdowns, and sometimes wildcat strikes to minimize the worst effects of the new system. Management will then introduce new measures to get around these responses, and workers will individually and collectively strive to create new ways to handle the new rules. A spiral of conflict emerges, with management seeing the workers as lazy and scheming and workers resisting those pressures and processes that treat them as wooden men and women. The struggle within the shop goes on continually, but it is a struggle in which the owners and managers hold most of the cards.

At the *public* level, when labor unions enter into negotiations with employers or press claims upon the government, the need for work reform is seldom a high-priority issue. But here, too, worker frustration with the conditions of work exerts its influence on those issues that are defined. The intensity with which unions press claims on those issues that can be legitimately defined within the system reflects in part the rage workers feel because of their inability to define the structure of work itself as a public issue of paramount importance. In our society, the politics of work is typically a sublimated politics.

The reasoning goes something like this: "Maybe we can't stop them from imposing inhumane work conditions on us, but they are going to have to pay for it with higher wages." Or: "Maybe we can't eliminate this mindless work, but we *can* struggle to make sure that the children of our race, sex, religion receive an opportunity to fill those few jobs that are satisfying." Or (think of medicine, law, professors, skilled crafts): "Everybody wants into our occupation because the others are so deadly, so we better organize to keep them out; if we don't we'll end up oversupplied with personnel and then *we'll* be ripe for the same routinization and authoritarian control they labor under." Or (think of truckers, assembly line workers, janitors, low-level bureaucrats): "Why should those professors and public bureaucrats have it so easy? Why shouldn't they punch a clock like we do?" Or (think of the same constituencies): "Why should welfare mothers get paid for sitting around; let them work like everybody else." The grievances reflected in these demands for *higher wages, equal opportunity, protective unionism*, and *punitive legislation* against privileged professions and the unemployed are certainly important in themselves within the established system of stratification. But other pressures are involved as well.

First, these are in part surrogate issues. If significant reform of work life were established in a variety of occupations, some of these issues would dissolve and the others would diminish in intensity. In this way the politics of work operates in the background of many of the political issues with which we are most familiar. Since workers cannot, it seems, make effective inroads on that fundamental issue (and the issue of inequality to which it is connected), they are more intensely committed in those surrogate issue areas where they can make a difference.[36]

Second, these are exactly the issues that divide working-class constituencies along racial, sexual, ethnic, and status lines. If the issue of work life reform which (to some extent) these constituencies share cannot be translated into a high-priority political issue, then the very factors that push the issue of work life reform out of the public arena also help to divide the working class into warring factions. The working class pays dearly for its failure to translate the need for work reform into a viable political issue.

Why haven't unions simply defined work reform as a basic demand, pressing the government and corporations to respond affirmatively? A full answer must await our discussion in the next section of the structural constraints within which proposals for work reform are confined. For now we can say that American trade unions respond to these restraints in a fairly consistent way. They can deliver on the rank-and-file desire for higher wages because the cost to management of concessions here can be transferred to consumers as higher prices. But management is more obstinate in dealing with demands for work reform; those reforms would threaten their control over the production process. A union that stakes everything on this issue would be likely to lose. It might also find itself losing the support of its own membership. Unions, then, often serve as a vehicle for converting work reform needs into proposals for wage increases, protectionism, and other fringe benefits. Because workers are always struggling to make ends meet in an inflationary economy, the workers themselves accept success in the available area rather than risk defeat in the unavailable one.

This displacement of issues is profoundly important in American politics. And through such processes the politics of work emerges as an indirect, sublimated politics punctuated periodically by local wildcat strikes.

So far, though, we have concentrated on the blue-collar worker and have used work on the assembly line as our paradigm of Taylorized work. Since only 2 percent of all American laborers work on the assembly line today and since the white-collar worker is increasingly prevalent in the work force, some critics will undoubtedly say that the issue of work reform will soon disappear without recourse to a political struggle. As the proportion of blue-collar workers steadily declines, the pertinence of work reform will decline steadily too, until Taylorism slides gracefully into history. That contention, in our view, is thoroughly mistaken. To challenge it we must look more closely at changes in the composition of the American work force.

Notice, first, the changing proportions of those who are self-employed and those who are dependent employees. In 1780, 20 percent of the labor force consisted of nonmanagerial employees, 80 percent were self-employed as farmers, merchants, lawyers, bankers, doctors, blacksmiths, and so on. By 1920 these figures were nearly reversed: 73 percent were nonmanagerial employees, 23.5 percent were self-employed, and 2.6 percent were classified as managerial employees. And by 1969, 83 percent were nonmanagerial wage and salary employees, only 9.2 percent were self-employed, and 7.2 percent were managerial officials. The first fact to note, then, is the massive shift in our work force from a middle class society of the self-employed to a society in which the dependent employee is the prevailing type. Today over 80 percent of all adults in the work force are dependent employees working in organizations that exert great influence over their pay, job security, and conditions of work.[37]

But these figures do not tell us how dependent employees are distributed among blue- and white-collar jobs. These internal changes are equally impressive: In 1870 white-collar workers made up 7 percent of the work force; by 1940 they made up 33 percent; by 1969, 47 percent. They will probably outnumber blue-collar workers by 50 percent in 1980. But accompanying this shift in the composition of the work force has been a corollary shift in the organization of work performed by white-collar workers. To speak of the first shift without attending closely to the second is to perpetuate a myth about white-collar work in America today.

We tend to think of white-collar work as work involving intellectual accomplishment, personal initiative, and some degree of managerial responsibility. But our image of the white-collar worker is drawn from the most prestigious, satisfying occupations within that category; in fact, most white-collar workers have more in common with blue-collar workers than they do with high-level administrators or technical experts. As C. Wright Mills put it in his classic study of the white-collar worker in the 1950s, "there are few, if any, features of wage work (except heavy toil, which is decreasingly a factor in wage work) that do not also characterize at least some white-collar work."[38]

Let us consider clerical and secretarial workers, by far the largest category in the white-collar force. If the old-fashioned bank clerk and private secretary were personally tied to their companies, if each had diverse and sometimes challenging responsibilities, that is decreasingly true today. In the modern office secretarial pools often replace the personal secretary. In the largest operations each of the classical secretarial functions—filing, typing, recording, taking notes—is assigned to different personnel, sometimes to different pools. Time-and-motion studies are then performed on these separate tasks, and "secretaries" find themselves increasingly assigned to repeat one detailed operation while meeting performance quotas established by management.

The contemporary equivalent of the traditional clerk is also subject to Taylorist forms of work and evaluation in the large bureaucracies of today. One investigator summarizes the division of tasks among "clerks" in a typical modern firm:

> Characteristically, separate clerks open the mail, date and route orders, interpret customer information, clear credit, check the items ordered for clarity . . . , extend discounts, calculate shipping charges, etc.[39]

The work of secretarial and clerical employees is thus more and more subject to Taylorist principles in the large private and public bureaucracies. We are, in fact, witnessing today the emergence of white-collar factories, in which paper and data processing resemble the automobile assembly line in many ways.

As we proceed to the more prestigious sectors of white-collar work, we can see similar pressures emerging. Thus the computer, according to the testimony of its early enthusiasts, was to eliminate a great deal of repetitive white-collar work while generating new positions for highly skilled white-collar employees. Today we do see an impressive array of computer operatives graded by pay and status. The upper-level jobs, that of the systems analyst and the computer programmer, carry some degree of autonomy, and these employees do exercise some imagination and responsibility in their work. But these characteristics recede as we move down to the more numerous computer console operators, key punch operators, tape librarians, and stockroom attendants. Workers in these areas experience a high degree of tension and boredom; their absenteeism and turnover rates are high; their promotion opportunities are slight.

Even programmers find their work less fulfilling than enthusiasts had anticipated. Listen to a 45-year-old programmer earning $18,000 a year (1974) describe, not what he can buy with his income, but what he gets out of his work:

> *I like the people I work with. Good people. . . . It's just that I don't care about it. I spend eight hours a day, five days a week, doing something I don't care about. . . . I'd like some sort of social work, programming in alcoholism research or drug addiction control. But that's hard to find. . . . I think up questions so that I can talk with people. Legitimate questions. But it's a game of mine to get out of work. I'm like a boxer in the ring. I go to the ropes. Pace. Drink water. But sooner or later I have to start punching again.*[40]

Here the problem is partly the work routine itself, but partly, too, the lack of valuable social purpose served by the work. This concern is voiced at all levels of the occupational system, as by the woman on the Lordstown assembly line who told an interviewer, "I would never buy a Chevy."[41] It is accentuated as a problem in many higher-status occupations where work schedules are not so thoroughly routinized but where the product or service itself lacks those qualities of social utility and craftsmanship in which one can take pride.

There are satisfying jobs sprinkled throughout the occupational system. Even some lower-income jobs have their advantages: The mechanic in the small shop, the teacher in the small community, the clerk in the bookshop often control the pace of their own work and perform services of intrinsic social importance. And these examples increase as we climb the occupational ladder: Technicians in highly automated and profitable industries such as oil refining and electrical equipment often have challenging work and a measure of control over their work environment. Indeed, because of their command of scarce skills and the favorable market position of their firms, such workers often press militantly and successfully for work reform. The professions of law, medicine, and college teaching also retain much of the autonomy and challenge that traditionally have made them favored professions for the sons and daughters of the middle class. Even here, though, the space within which these professionals work is increasingly subject to segmentation, performance quotas, and control by administrative personnel less thoroughly committed to the integrity of the profession.

The problem is this: The very jobs that challenge one's abilities, engage one's interest, and serve a social purpose worthy of personal commitment become, in a society where most work lacks these characteristics, the occupational targets towards which increasing numbers of young people understandably aim. The result is an over-supply of talent that threatens to drain the oases as everybody flees the desert. As individuals strive to locate fulfilling work in an occupational system dominated by Taylorism, Taylorism itself moves into new occupational outposts. And though important differences do exist, the grievances and aspirations of most dependent employees move increasingly in the same direction. Their common grievances reflect dependence within an occupational system oriented toward managerial prerogatives and private profit and away from worker prerogatives and community welfare. Listen to a medley of voices convey the frustrations and aspirations of the dependent employee:

THE PROJECT COORDINATOR: *Gradually your effectiveness wears down. Pretty soon, you no longer identify as the bright guy with the ideas. You become a fly in the ointment. You're criticized by your superiors and your subordinates not in a direct manner. Indirectly, by being ignored.*

THE STOCKBROKER: *In this rip-off, we're treated with contempt by members of the stock exchange. They're really saying, "If you make too big a noise, we're gonna have a girl take the orders and the machine'll do the rest. . . ."*

THE BUREAUCRAT: *They get what they want out of people by threatening them economically. It makes people apple polishers and ass kissers. I used to hear people say "work needs to be redefined." I thought they were crazy. Now I know they're not.*

THE FIREMAN: *I worked in a bank. You know it's just paper. It's not real. Nine to five and it's shit. . . . But the firemen, you actually see them produce. You see them put out a fire. You see them come out with babies in their hands. . . . I can look back and say "I helped put out that fire. . . ." It shows something I did on this earth.*

THE UNION LEADER AT LORDSTOWN: *A unimate is a welding robot. . . . If the guys didn't stand up and fight, they'd become robots too.* [42]

Blue- and white-collar workers sing the same song but with different voices and intonations. As dependent employees, they share thwarted aspirations for challenging, engaging, and purposeful work pursued in democratic settings. The politics of work will become a more public, militant politics when dependent employees in a variety of occupations begin to subordinate their differences in status, education, and pay levels to shared interests in reconstituting power relations and routines within the work place itself.

The Prospects for Work Reform

The prevailing idea of work in our society is so deeply embedded in our production processes that it is easy to think of it as the only possible form, insusceptible to reformulation. We become resigned to necessity. Even our language reflects this sense of necessity and resignation. Thus we think of play and leisure as relatively trivial activities pursued for their own sakes; and we think of work, by comparison, as a more serious endeavor, inherently distasteful and pursued as a necessary means to feed our families, secure a better life for our children, and provide us with time for play and leisure. These categories fit much of our actual experience, but they also distort our perception of alternative styles emerging in certain occupations and potential alternatives inherent in others. If some find their work intrinsically satisfying, they tend to deny or understate it for fear that others will think they are being paid for playing. If others contemplate work reform in stultifying jobs, they are charged with wanting to play for money. Our *categories* themselves reflect Taylor's view that "it is a matter of ordinary common sense to plan working hours so that workers can really 'work while they work' and 'play while they play.' "[43] If the distinction between work and play could only be drawn in this way, common sense would also be good sense. But we must not allow our thought to be dominated by the Taylorist assumptions embedded in our language. Work *can* be nontrivial, demanding, instrumental, and intrinsically fulfilling all at the same time. To revise received distinctions in this way is to heighten our ability to bring a critical perspective to bear on alienating work routines; we expand our sense of the possible by reminding ourselves that Taylorist distinctions between work and leisure are not etched in stone.

Work as we know it is not work as it has always been practiced and known. For the early Greeks, work, *ponos*, was physical activity that was drudgery, a burden; the word itself was derived from the

Greek word for sorrow. In feudal society the purpose of work was closely linked to God's will and purpose; one worked out of Christian charity or as a remedy for temptation. And while many were ground down by heavy labor, the prevailing model of work was provided by the idea of craftsmanship. Labor, as we define and measure it, was an alien idea; there was no unit of labor time as we know it today. Work and leisure, effort and pride, production and social life, were organically connected. The long hours of the craftsman were not strictly hours of labor time, because social relations were embedded in work relations. The "awareness of being part of a large social community permeated the work place, and the awareness of belonging to an occupational community dominated social relations of the job."[44] One does not have to understate the hard life faced by the peasant and the craftsman to perceive that work as they knew it was quite unlike work as we know it.

The ideas and forms of work prevailing at any time reflect and help to shape the entire society within which they exist. Put another way, significant changes in the structure of work must be accompanied by corollary changes in scientific knowledge, technological possibilities, educational institutions, moral codes, and patterns of political expectation. If work as we know it at this point in history is once again open to reconstitution, it can only be because a broad set of economic and social institutions are undergoing, or potentially open to, structural change.

To ask, What are the prospects for work reform? is to ask, What broader changes encourage or stifle a redefinition of the work ethic and a reconstitution of work processes? If the need for reform has persisted at least as long as Taylorism has flourished, what factors, if any, make it more possible to speak to that need today?

Consider, first, a set of tendencies that undermine the legitimacy of the old work ethic and provide potential openings for work reform.

1. Governments in Sweden and Yugoslavia, where work reform has gained a foothold, also have a commitment to the maintenance of full employment. Under these conditions managers cannot easily use the threat of unemployment to discipline the labor force; they must explore new incentives to enhance worker productivity. In Sweden the problems of absenteeism, turnover, and idleness did encourage management to experiment with modest work reform schemes. Extensive unemployment, then, tends to suppress the issue of work reform, since the workers' first priority is to seek or retain jobs. But when organized labor secures a viable policy of full employment, it creates one of the preconditions for work reform. If

employment levels vary significantly across occupational categories, as they do in the United States, we can expect those in highly skilled, undersupplied occupations to have more leverage with respect to conditions of work than those in low-skilled, oversupplied areas. But even these differences in opportunities will be reduced if any large portion of the work force is insecure. For, as we have already noted, the sons and daughters of those in marginal jobs will strive to enter the more rewarding occupations, inflating the supply and increasing the hazards of unemployment at these levels. Thus a society with stable full employment is more open to pressure for work reform than one with high unemployment (or underemployment) in any areas.

2. In a similar way, a political economy that can and does control inflation is more likely to place work reform high on its agenda. For if inflation eats away at incomes, workers must struggle to gain comparable pay increases, thereby pushing work reform to a lower position on their priority list. Moreover, if a political economy oscillates, as ours does, between periods of high unemployment and high inflation, the oscillation itself will limit workers' ability to translate the need for work reform into a viable political demand.

3. As the educational level of the working population improves, it is encouraged to expect work opportunities commensurate with its talents and its abilities to assume responsibility. The gap in the United States between the educational levels of the employee force and the intellectual demands of the jobs available in the occupational system creates space within which worker frustration expands and pressures for work reform grow. This uneven development between the educational and occupational systems helped to explode the myth of the happy worker in the late 1960s.

4. As the production system has matured, spewing out consumer goods in massive varieties and amounts, it has been necessary to accelerate consumer demand for goods through advertising. But such luxury advertising, to be effective, must appeal to the carefree life, the life of sexual liaisons, casual attitudes, self-indulgence. And luxury advertising, even though it is a requirement of the marketing system, almost certainly helps to undermine the instrumental work ethic central to the production system. This contradiction in modern capitalism is expressed as one imperative toward self-discipline and another toward self-indulgence; it surely encourages people to look upon the conditions of work with a critical eye. Burdens and grievances that were present all along now become more sharply defined and less acceptable.[45]

5. If the threats of unemployment and inflation have helped to discipline a labor force subjected to Taylorism, the promise of future affluence has played its role too. Under Taylorism, the only function work has for the worker is to provide a means to subsistence and to affluence. But the promise of affluence seems to operate better as an incentive when its payoff is projected into the distant future: "We are working (struggling, sacrificing) today so that our children will have a better (more affluent) life tomorrow." By now, though, the sons and daughters of the upper-middle classes have tasted that promised affluence. And a crucial ingredient in the radicalism of the 1960s was the reaction of these young people against material opulence, environmental waste, and spiritual emptiness. Delivery on the promise of affluence has accentuated the lack of meaning and purpose in a materialist culture; the goal itself loses its ability to motivate and energize the young. Such a reaction must alter attitudes toward work. When people say they lack purpose and meaning in work, they mean in part that the old purpose and meaning—work as a means to affluence—has lost its significance. Affluence is shallow; it cannot serve as a viable incentive to mindless, repetitive work for those who have tasted its fruits. Thus delivery on the promise of affluence helps to undermine the very work ethic that contributed to its delivery.[46]

If, as many studies suggest, meaningful work reform often increases productivity, and if the factors mentioned before—full employment, low inflation, worker absenteeism, higher educational attainment of young workers, modern forms of advertising, and the shallowness of affluence—all seem to point toward work reform, why don't the pressures for reform become irresistible? What or who stands in the way of changes that would benefit the entire society?

There are, first of all, structural factors in the economy. If the inflation and unemployment spiral is endemic to contemporary American capitalism, then these forces will press against work reform. In that respect alone, the preconditions for work reform include the displacement of the economic system that repeatedly traps its workers in an inflation-unemployment spiral.

There are also technological limitations. Many industries have large investments in technologies organized around Taylorist principles. Marginal or declining industries (the auto industries are in the latter category) might have to limp along with the technologies they now have, making some work reform possible but significant change difficult. This obstacle, though, is not in itself insuperable throughout the economy.

More important is the fact that several of the factors noted before (educated workers, luxury advertising, and disillusion with affluence) have emerged relatively recently in the American political economy. And each of the elements is structurally related to the others. Thus a trend in the opposite direction is certainly possible. We could experience a long-term decline in employment, a decline in advertising aimed at self-indulgence, a reversal of educational opportunities for many Americans, and a decline in affluence. The need for a reconstitution of work would remain, but the political opportunities to promote it would be absent. The situation would not be exactly as we knew it, say in the 1920s and 1950s, for the population, having experienced and lost affluence, would be embittered by false promises. They would also be more alert to the limits posed by the environment to the endless pursuit of affluence. Threats and coercive pressure would then play a central role in disciplining those segments of the work force oppressed by Taylorism. But in the short run, at least, work reform probably would be subordinated to more pressing issues, even by socialists.

The pressures we have so far noted operate together to pose powerful obstacles to meaningful work reform within the present system. They are in fact so powerful because of internal instabilities within the capitalist system of political economy. But there are related pressures that demonstrate even more dramatically the contradiction between significant work reform and the maintenance of an economic system fueled by the private profits of private owners. These pressures show socialism to be a necessary, though not sufficient, condition of unalienating work for most working people.

Corporate owners and managers are alert to the studies in management journals connecting work reform to improved productivity. Why have most been extremely hesitant to act? Because the reforms that would decrease worker alienation and increase productivity pose a threat initially to managerial prerogatives and eventually to the system of private ownership itself. Corporate control over the work force would be jeopardized if jobs were redesigned and if channels of participation and information were opened. Recall, for instance, how the Carnegie Steel Company in 1892 reduced its dependence on skilled craftsmen in order to increase its control over the work process (see Chapter 3). A production process that engages skilled, knowledgeable workers creates a set of irreplaceable workers; if *they* lobby government or strike, owners and politicians must listen carefully. Meaningful work reform, in short, would make a larger number of workers in a variety of occupations less dispensable and more powerful. If they later challenged the prerogatives of managers and owners, they would have a more effective power base from which to launch the challenge.

But of course the connections we see between work reform and a threat to the private corporate system cannot serve as a motive for corporate opposition to work reform unless corporate elites themselves see it this way. They do. Though it would be impolitic for them to emphasize the point—it would feed the flames of worker discontent—enough signals have been given in publications read primarily by corporate and financial elites to get the message out.[47] We cite one example.

Thomas Fitzgerald, director of employee research and training activities at the Chevrolet Division, General Motors, published an essay in the *Harvard Business Review* in 1971, responding to those managerial theorists who have argued in favor of work reform. His essay is entitled "Why Motivation Theory Won't Work," and its contents are quite interesting.[48]

Fitzgerald acknowledges that American corporations face growing problems with worker absenteeism, turnover, idleness, featherbedding, and product defects. He agrees that these problems have provided impetus for a lively literature in business journals favorable to work reform. The authors don't always distinguish carefully enough, Fitzgerald notes, between those reforms that would increase worker *satisfaction* and those that would improve their *motivation* to work. The two may not always go together, and management, he implies, should be primarily interested in the latter.

He then contends that the problem of motivation is embedded in the structure of contemporary industrial society. The old work ethic is in trouble, and the classical sanction of unemployment is "partly neutralized by a full-employment welfare system and the protections possible for individuals through combinations (unions)."[49]

A number of traits once common to workers ("orderliness, punctuality . . . , success striving, deference to rank and authority, predictability . . . , reliance on rules and procedures")[50] are no longer to be taken for granted. But then Fitzgerald expresses skepticism about work reforms designed to cope with these changes in worker "traits." Over the long term the beneficial effects of "job enlargement" are likely to wear off just as the effects of increased pay schedules did (he says) in an earlier period. Also, managerial flexibility in "reallocating unskilled labor without loss of training investment would be reduced" if such reforms were introduced.[51] And since one job enlargement is likely to lead to another, managers should be hesitant in starting down this road.

He is even more wary of worker participation in decision making. First, he thinks, it won't succeed. He assumes, as early opponents to political democracy did, that workers will be too apathetic. More important, if it did work, it would lead to a challenge of traditional managerial prerogatives. Fitzgerald is eloquent on this point:

> *Once competence is shown (or believed to be shown) in, say, rearranging the work area, and after participation has become a conscious, officially sponsored activity, participators may well want to go on to topics of job assignment, the allocation of rewards, or even the selection of leadership. In other words, management's present monopoly—on initiating participation, on the nomination of conferees, and on the limitation of legitimate areas for review—can itself easily become a source of contention.* [52]

Meaningful work reform, Fitzgerald agrees, would involve job redesign, worker participation in the decision process, and worker access to the requisite information for intelligent participation. But inroads in these areas would increase the power and indispensability of workers while decreasing managerial monopoly over information and power. Once this process is started, it could easily get out of hand. So it is best not to allow it to start. "History," Fitzgerald warns, "does not offer many examples of oligarchies that have abdicated with grace and goodwill." [53]

For Fitzgerald these considerations constitute an argument for corporate opposition to work reform. Acknowledging difficulty in motivating the contemporary worker, but refusing to sanction work reform, he calls instead for a series of gimmicks within the present system of work, such as company recreation teams, contests, slogans, and managerial praise of workers with desirable traits.

The owning and managerial classes, entrenched in the most developed capitalist system in the world, will firmly oppose work reform that threatens their power base and prerogatives. They will oppose, that is, meaningful work reform. But if work reform is desirable in itself, and if it is connected to other important objectives like reducing inequality and establishing environmental integrity, then the issue of work reform must not be allowed to languish. Those pressures and elites within the capitalist political economy that obstruct work reform actually provide a case not for the retention of Taylorism, inequality, environmental degradation, and wage-price cycles, but for socialism. Although socialism does not guarantee that work reform and other objectives will be achieved, it is a crucial precondition for their promotion.

NOTES

1. The employer's purpose in designing work, we will argue, is to promote the highest efficiency of the worker compatible with the employer's ability to retain a high level of control over the work process. These two objectives are closely connected to the goal of private profit maximized over the long run. We return to this issue in our discussion of Taylorism.

2. Reported in *Work in America*, Special Task Force Report to the Department of Health, Education and Welfare (Cambridge: M.I.T. Press, 1973), p. 14.

3. *The Affluent Worker* (London: Cambridge University Press, 1968), I: 108–109.

4. "The Politics of Consensus in an Age of Affluence," *American Political Science Review* (December 1965). During periods of affluence "men feel more in control of their lives" (p. 879).

5. Ibid., pp. 879–880. The science from which Mills and Fromm were alienated, and to which Lane and Goldthorpe were committed, was the study of public attitudes through surveys.

6. The report of this incident is taken from Andre Gorz, "Workers Control Is More Than Just That," in *Workers Control*, ed. Gerry Hunnius, G. David Garson, and John Case (New York: Vintage Books, 1973), pp. 325–343.

7. These examples are also detailed in Gorz, pp. 334–335.

8. A summary of the strike can be found in David Jenkins, *Job Power* (Baltimore: Penguin Books, 1974), ch. 9.

9. Quoted in Emma Rothschild, *Paradise Lost: The Decline of the Auto-Industrial Age* (New York: Vintage Books, 1974), p. 100. Another excellent treatment of the Lordstown struggles is found in Stanley Aronowitz, *False Promises* (New York: McGraw-Hill, 1973), ch. 1.

10. Quoted in Jenkins, p. 51.

11. The income, status, and educational level attached to a job is partly a function of the skill level and autonomy the job allows. It is not surprising that these factors cannot easily be unsorted, since a significant change in one requires significant changes in the others. These studies are summarized in *Work in America*, pp. 16, 76–93.

12. The distinction is important: The former asks how workers can achieve jobs and working conditions that engage their capacities and interests in fulfilling ways. The concern with worker motivation asks only how the worker can be made more efficient and reliable. If

discipline and narrow job assignments prove more effective than fulfilling work, then they are judged to be the better motivators, regardless of the effects on the workers.

13. More careful, in-depth surveys can probe beneath this surface, but it is essential that survey analysts be exposed thoroughly to *alternative* theories, which they would seek to test during the interviews. It helps too, of course, if they are aware of how work is organized differently in other societies and ask workers to compare their actual experiences to likely experiences under those conditions. And, of course, individual interviews should be supplemented with group interviews. Then the interview technique can be of some limited value, still to be complemented by other modes of inquiry.

14. Taylor, *The Principles of Scientific Management* (1911) (New York: Norton, 1967), p. 47.

15. Ibid., p. 130.

16. Ibid., p. 36.

17. Ibid., p. 25.

18. Ibid., p. 26.

19. Ibid., p. 39.

20. Ibid., p. 95.

21. Ibid., p. 125.

22. Ibid., p. 120.

23. *Democracy in America* ed. Richard D. Heffner (New York: Mentor Books, 1956), pp. 217–218.

24. We draw upon the translation in Erich Fromm (ed.), *Marx's Concept of Man* (New York: Ungar, 1961). It is not our intent to ask whether the theory of alienation is still present in Marx's later work. The affirmative view has been defended by Shlomo Avineri, *The Social Thought of Karl Marx* (London: Cambridge University Press, 1970), and denied by Louis Althusser, *For Marx* (New York: Vintage Books, 1970). We suspect that Marx revised his earlier ideas about alienation but that in revised form they continued to play a role in his mature theory.

25. *Marx's Concept of Man*, p. 101.

26. Karl Marx, *The Grundrisse*, ed. and trans. David McClellan (New York: Harper Torchbooks, 1972), p. 124.

27. *Marx's Concept of Man*, p. 101.

28. Ibid., p. 97.

29. Ibid., p. 204.

30. Ibid., p. 214.

31. Our thinking on the subject is summarized in two essays collected in William Connolly and Glen Gordon (eds.), *Social Structure and Political Theory* (Lexington, Mass.: Heath, 1974): Steven Lukes, "Alienation and Anomie," pp. 192–211; and Connolly, "Theoretical Self-Consciousness," pp. 40–67.

32. See the experiments summarized in *Work in America*, pp. 188–201, and in Jenkins, *Job Power*.

33. It is not always between workers and owners, but in the public sector between workers and controllers. We agree, of course, that alienating work can emerge in societies where private ownership is absent and centralized planning prevails. We will return to this question in the last chapter, where we consider the connections between planning and freedom. For now it is sufficient to say that our society is *objectively* in a better position than any in the world to promote unalienating work, since most socialist societies are at much earlier stages of accumulation than we are. Hence the key question is: What forces operate in our system to obstruct changes that are objectively possible? The dismal view that every evil manifest in our society also happens to be a requirement of industrial organization or human nature itself is one that has been popular with apologists throughout history (think of the defenses of slavery, the subordination of women, the early arguments against political democracy). In fact, the early arguments against political democracy had very much the same structure as contemporary arguments against industrial democracy.
34. Quoted in *Work in America*, p. 13.
35. Quoted in William F. Whyte et al. (eds.), *Money and Motivation* (New York: Harper and Row, 1955), p. 15.
36. The process by which more fundamental grievances that are illegitimate in the prevailing system are converted into less fundamental issues that are legitimate is crucial to the understanding of our system of issue formation and resolution. The best place to start in thinking about this process is E. E. Schattschneider, *The Semisovereign People* (New York: Holt, Rinehart and Winston, 1960), especially ch. 4, "The Displacement of Conflicts."
37. These figures and the following ones are from Michael Reich, "The Evolution of the United States Working Force," in *The Capitalist System,* ed. Richard Edwards, Michael Reich, Thomas Weiskopf (Englewood Cliffs, N.J.: Prentice Hall, 1972), pp. 174–183.
38. *White Collar* (New York: Oxford University Press, 1951), p. 227.
39. Harry Braverman, "Labor and Monopoly Capital," *Monthly Review* (July-August 1974), p. 67. Our treatment of all workers in the white-collar category is indebted to this essay as well as to Braverman's book *Labor and Monopoly Capital* (New York: Monthly Review Press, 1974).
40. Interview in the *Boston Globe*, December 2, 1974.
41. The interviewer is Emma Rothschild in *Paradise Lost*, p. 96.
42. These quotations are excerpted from Studs Terkel's superb study *Working* (New York: Pantheon Books, 1972), pp. 341, 340, 347, 589, and 91, respectively.
43. Taylor, p. 87.
44. Edward Shorter, "The History of Work in the West," in *Work and Community in the West* (New York: Harper Torchbooks, 1973), p. 9. For a brief survey of changes in the idea of work over the ages, see

Adriano Tilgher, *Homo Faber: Work Through the Ages* (Chicago: Regnery, 1930).

45. Of course, if the production system were more fully oriented to pressing social needs, it would not be so dependent on manipulative advertising. There would be a ready use and market for its goods. It is, then, the false priorities in production that require the expensive advertising, and the advertising then helps to generate criticisms against the production processes.

46. The argument that there is a "motivation crisis" emerging within advanced capitalism is developed by Jurgen Habermas in *Legitimation Crisis* (Boston: Beacon Press, 1974).

47. Public statements by corporate elites and sometimes managerial theorists are often part of the politics of work. While proponents of work reform seek to mobilize workers, proponents of the status quo must seek to immobilize them. They will thus temper public statements that might arouse the opposition. Their public statements must then be decoded with our understanding of such political considerations firmly in mind.

48. *Harvard Business Review* (July-August, 1971), pp. 37–43.

49. Ibid., p. 39.

50. Ibid., p. 40.

51. Ibid., p. 41.

52. Ibid., p. 43.

53. Ibid.

The Crisis
of the State

The Symptoms and the Illness

A state and a government are not the same thing.[1] Two countries could have the same form of government (for instance, a presidential system or parliamentary system, a democracy or republic) but differ in the form of the state. England and the United States, for instance, both have democratic governments in the narrow sense that the public officials in each are selected through competitive elections, but England has a more developed welfare state. To speak of government is to refer to the institutions through which public decisions are made, the rules that govern the decision makers, the way officials are selected and replaced, and so on. The state includes the government, but it also refers to the range of institutions and practices that are incorporated into public life. The sphere of the state is the sphere of public authority and power. A public university is not part of the government in the United States but it is part of the state. In some societies religion is part of the state, whereas in others, such as the United States, religious life remains in the private sphere. Most important for our purposes, some states fully incorporate economic institutions while others primarily enforce contracts, leaving most other aspects of the economy to the private sector.

States differ in the areas brought under public control and in the ways the areas are incorporated. A *laissez-faire state* minimizes the public role in economic transactions and maximizes the private. Economic transactions are left in the hands of private proprietors; the state merely enforces contracts, apprehends and punishes criminals, controls the legitimate means of military and police violence, and perhaps guarantees the protection of certain civil liberties. The *positive* (or *welfare*) *state* expands the public role in economic transactions. While leaving the ownership of productive enterprises primarily in the private sphere, it assumes some responsibility for promoting broad economic objectives such as full employment and low inflation; supports capitalist production by public expenditures for highways, military, airports, research, education of technicians and the like; tries (with varying degrees of seriousness) to meet social needs unmet by the system of private production through programs such as health insurance, public housing, job training, social security, unemployment insurance, and relief payments; and sometimes acquires ownership of economic units (such as railroads or utilities) that are essential to the economic system but not (or no longer) profitable to private owners. The *socialist state* owns the crucial productive enterprises, and as we use the term, it also places high priority on reducing economic inequality among its citizens and on promoting public, collective products and services (mass transit systems, public education, parks, health care units) over the private, individualized products more typical of private enterprise. Democratic socialism, as we construe it, is a socialist state in which, first, the major public institutions, including government and corporations, are subject to public participation and accountability and, second, in which the sharp distinctions between people who do mental and executive work and others who do only mindless work are significantly narrowed. It is fair to say that while only a few welfare states approximate the ideals embodied in their justifying rhetorics (for instance, Sweden, but not the United States), no contemporary socialist state approximates the ideal of democratic socialism. With respect to the welfare state and the socialist state, we can ask, Can the stated ideals of each be promoted adequately, given the *legitimate means* available to the state in each system? Are the ideals themselves justified? Having answered the second question earlier with respect to corporate capitalism through our exploration of work life and inequality, we will now pay special attention to the first. Our primary attention will be focused on the welfare state in the United States, which given its crucial military and economic role in the "free world" and the distinctive way in which it has developed the institution of corporate capitalism, is not completely comparable to welfare states in other capitalist societies.[2] It is only if these questions are answered negatively with respect to the welfare state that the corollary questions about democratic socialism assume a similar importance.

The positive state, or the welfare state, as we will call it in accordance with conventional usage in the United States, can only be understood within the larger context of corporate capitalism. Given the *public responsibilities* assumed by the welfare state and the narrow range of *ideological debate* prevailing in the United States between liberals and business conservatives, the structural defects and dislocations of corporate capitalism are widely if misleadingly interpreted as defects in the welfare state itself. The legitimacy of the welfare state is indeed being questioned, because of many recent crises, but the crises are not wholly of its own making. It suffers from the fact that it is publicly accountable for the performance of the economy while its resources for coping with that performance are severely limited. Corporate owners, meanwhile, pursue policies that affect the life chances of citizens without being held publicly accountable for the outcomes. Behind the symptoms of welfare state malaise lies the illness of corporate capitalism; the medicine used to treat the symptoms exacerbates the illness and further undermines public support for the welfare state.

The politics of the welfare state, which is a politics of *interest protection* for owners and privileged beneficiaries of the means of production, is, in many ways, a politics of *interest displacement* for the working class and the underclass. Unemployed workers, lacking the means to hold corporate owners accountable, demand that the state create jobs in the private sector. Underemployed blacks and women, unable to secure better jobs from business, plead for state subsidies to see them through. Victims of spiraling inflation, unable to curb the style changes, product priorities, and price markups of the corporate system, vote out government officials who fail to bring price spirals under control. Working-class taxpayers, subsidizing both the corporate structure and those left without jobs in the corporate system, demand cuts in the welfare budget to ease the squeeze on the family budget. Blacks and whites, unable to expand the limited supply of decent jobs in the corporate system, compete over available prizes while colliding in the public arena over the issues of busing and affirmative action. Commuters, breathing toxic fumes in daily traffic jams, accept the privately profitable and socially costly system of automobile transportation while demanding more public highways to ease the worst jams.

Since production and profit taking are concentrated in the private sphere and public problem solving and accountability in the state, the public issues that are defined do not squarely address the injuries that are done. This is the politics of displacement. The welfare state responds to these displaced pressures within the limits legitimately available to it. Thus, especially during good times, it deflates the pressures through public programs that give private owners incentive to invest while introducing marginal forms of security (social security, unemployment insurance, jobs in the military) for those not included in the expansionary drive. Or, especially during hard times, drawing on repressive elements like the police, the prisons, and the military, it intimidates, isolates, and controls those with grievances while cutting back or stabilizing public welfare programs in the name of fiscal responsibility. Both responses swell the size of the public sector in nonproductive areas, thereby limiting the future options of the welfare state when the next wave of displaced pressures emerge. The welfare state in this way contributes to its own loss of legitimacy. Behind the ineffectiveness of government programs, worker resentment of welfare recipients, heightened racial tensions, declining constituency support for the liberal ideology of the New Deal and the Great Society, and the crisis of legitimacy for the welfare state itself lie fundamental irrationalities in the relation between the economy and the state required by the political economy of corporate capitalism.

If the symptoms continue to be construed widely as the illness itself, a protofascist reaction to the binds of corporate capitalism may emerge. Those teetering on the edge of insecurity will support repressive control against those already pushed over the edge in the hope that they can thus avoid the plunge themselves. But if the deeper dimensions of contemporary dislocations and malaise receive a wider airing, one preliminary condition for the transition from the welfare state to the democratic socialist state will be secured. That, in summary form, is our thesis. Its underpinnings will now be elaborated.

The Paralyzed Economy

A *structural constraint* occurs when of two desirable outcomes, X and Y, neither can be promoted without limiting the attainment of the other. Sometimes it is possible, as Keynesians showed in the early 1960s with respect to high employment and low inflation, to promote through public policy a tradeoff situation so that each is promoted to some degree but neither so completely that it undermines attainment of the other. A *structural contradiction* occurs when different aspects of established practices collide in such a way that both X and Y suffer, sometimes so thoroughly that actions designed to promote one undermine both. A *bind* occurs when people in their roles as citizens, consumers, and workers are trapped by constraints and contradictions beyond their control. They can find no viable way out. A bind is the human dimension of structural constraints and contradictions. Often the pleas and demands that binds generate lead to policies that exacerbate the underlying dislocations. But sometimes, if more rarely, emerging awareness of the structural source of troubles generates support for needed institutional changes. The American political economy is beset by structural constraints, some of which increasingly approach the level of contradictions. Its citizens, but especially members of its subordinate classes, are increasingly trapped in binds. These pressures fuel the crisis of the welfare state.

1. The business cycle, once assuming the form of a structural constraint in which the government could choose either low inflation or low unemployment but not both, has acquired new dimensions. Capitalism needs healthy financial markets to grow, but capitalist growth undermines healthy financial markets. Capitalism needs profits to grow, but capitalist growth squeezes profits. It is necessary for government to maintain the liquidity of large corporations even when their debt is overextended and their profit margins are squeezed, but the deflationary tools formerly available to it in times of inflation (for instance, slowdown in the expansion of money, an increase in interest rates) cannot now be so freely used. These deflationary tools would further undermine corporate liquidity. This, combined with other factors discussed in Chapter 2, contributes to a merging of inflation and high unemployment in corporate capitalism and to a progressive weakening of government tools. From the vantage point of the breadwinner the struggle for security is now fought on several fronts at once: Inflation, increased federal, state, and local taxes, and increased job insecurity hit together.

2. The private transportation complex, made up of automobile, oil, trucking, highway construction, steel, tire, and glass companies, provided much of the momentum for corporate expansion and economic growth from the 1920s to the early part of the 1960s. But today the glutted market for cars can no longer grow substantially; the energy waste, air pollution, and urban deterioration flowing from widespread dependence on cars, trucks, and highways has dampened public enthusiasm for the established transportation system. But the private corporations involved, with massive investments in the old system, cannot easily afford to convert to bus and mass transit production. That would require a lot of new investment without the assurance of the former huge markets. It would even threaten to undermine what is left of the old market. The established production system, built on rapid product turnover, indefinitely expanding markets, and yearly style changes, retains too large a contemporary market to justify its dismantling, too small a market to promote the earlier rates of economic growth. The automobile-industrial complex, controlled by the imperatives of private profit, is caught in a bind: It can neither retool nor flourish in its present form. Its new circumstances, reminiscent of the situation facing the British steel industry at the turn of the century, symbolize some of the differences between a developing corporate economy in the first decades of the twentieth century and the mature corporate economy of the 1970s. But more than mere symbolism is involved. Since the automobile-industrial complex employs such a large portion of the labor force, its moribund status contributes decisively to the malaise of the whole economy. In the present system one fears that expanded military production is the easiest way to take up the slack.

3. The corporate system of production (expanding as it must) has steadily undermined the family as a *unit of production*, because *household* provision of clothing, equipment repair, gardening for food, care of the elderly, health care, recreation, and child care has given way increasingly to *corporate* production of those goods and services. The family costs of plugging into the established social system have therefore escalated. Corporate services, originally introduced to serve the needs of an affluent minority, tend eventually to become necessities for all citizens. The result is a decline in the family's ability to provide security and other social needs, an increase in wage demands, and an expansion of subsidies from the state. These in turn increase corporate costs of production in labor and taxes, and the corporation with a multinational capacity is encouraged to invest funds or move operations abroad to escape these

cost pressures. The final result may be to increase the threat of unemployment for many at the same time that consumption needs have expanded and private protections against insecurity have contracted.[3]

4. Individual mobility, idealized through the myth of equal opportunity, is essential to the political economy of corporate capitalism. Since the unplanned economic system develops unevenly—allowing some geographic areas to flourish while others languish, expanding the need for some occupations and skills while rendering others economically useless—it must have a labor force ready and willing ("free") to move when and where the system dictates. But the high rate of mobility, and its historical flow from the countryside to the city, undermines the integrity of extended kinship ties, neighborhoods, and large communities. The family, no longer a *productive unit* and now also less viable as a *social unit*, becomes primarily a *child-rearing* unit. The social ties that bind the individual to larger collectives are weakened. Women, isolated in the home, move into the labor market, accentuating the tendencies toward unemployment already present in the system. Women join blacks in the competition for scarce jobs, sometimes deepening class conflict as some middle-class white families have two breadwinners while some lower-class black families have none. Within the established context, the rational and liberal thing to press for would be state policies that encourage growth and expand job opportunities available in the corporate sector. The uneven development of employment opportunities further contribute to the breakdown of established social units without creating functional alternatives.[4]

5. A reduction in economic inequality, which is an important precondition for resolving collective problems generated by corporate capitalism, cannot proceed very far as long as corporate capitalism itself prevails. Capitalist growth depends on the rich to provide the savings necessary for capital accumulation. Moreover, the system needs the threat of unemployment for workers in the most menial jobs and the incentive of relatively high pay for those in jobs of greater responsibility. Inequality is necessary to keep people at work in the unfulfilling jobs available in corporate capitalism; it contributes to the control of the work force. The absence of opportunities to reduce inequality shifts political pressure to the faulty ideal of equal *opportunity* in a system of extensive inequality of *result*. Thus not only are urgent collective needs such as environmental control rendered less attainable by inequality but displaced pressures for equal opportunity foster social atomization.

6. It is in the *collective interest* of the owners of capital to reduce environmental degradation. Otherwise the natural support systems necessary to production will deteriorate, increasing costs of production and making some forms of production impossible. But *individual firms* find it unprofitable to introduce the needed controls unilaterally, while the collective reforms that are workable would require extensive revision of the system of corporate capitalism itself. Corporate capitalism requires economic growth to sustain investment and to fill new consumer needs created by the side effects of established practices, but a viable environmental policy probably requires a reallocation of resources and a slowing of cumulative growth. Similarly, a favorable setting for environmental reform could be promoted through a reduction in inequality, reform in the structure of work, and policies that encourage the growth of stable communities, but each of these changes is at odds with the established tendencies of corporate capitalism.

7. A reconstitution of work life might help to dampen wage demands in the corporate sector, increase worker productivity, and create one of the conditions for viable democratic participation in other areas of society. .Some of these possible effects, indeed, encouraged liberal managers to flirt with modest proposals for work reform in the 1960s. But meaningful work reform would involve workers in decision making, intruding on the private pursuit of profits; it would provide the worker with skills indispensable to the production process, thereby increasing collective worker leverage in labor negotiations and strikes. Work reform, needed to promote some objectives of corporate capitalism, is incompatible with others. Within the framework of this system, then, we must expect a cycle of modest experiments and idealism followed by managerial "realism" and disenchantment with work reform.

8. .An increasing number of young people, educated at universities, seek careers consonant with their intellectual development and social needs. But capitalism encourages authoritarian work relations and routinized work processes even at relatively high levels of the occupational system. The supply of aspirants outstrips the supply of good jobs. Since many of these young people know from the experience of their parents that affluence is not sufficient to promote the good life, their incentive to compete and work under the prevailing conditions is weakened. The goals of young people are increasingly at odds with the imperatives of the system; and while many "adjust" to these imperatives, the fund of good will and civility that previously tied the middle class to the system is depleted.

9. Though all American citizens require a defense establishment

to provide security, we do not all need a warfare state. The warfare state is required to protect the corporate empire abroad and to create demand for corporate products without undermining corporate control of the work force. But world reaction to the warfare state now threatens universal destruction or the return to universal barbarism. The United States sells massive amounts of military equipment abroad to offset a balance-of-payments problem, increasing the likelihood of war.[5] It exports nuclear technology as part of its policy to reduce the need of other countries for Arab oil and because it is profitable to do so. But a nuclear power plant creates a capacity for nuclear weapons, and the proliferation of nuclear weapons greatly increases the chances for secret attacks against the imperial power itself. The Maginot Line approach to nuclear deterrence becomes increasingly futile, while the size of our deterrent force requires other countries to expand their own. These tendencies, partly rooted in the anarchy of international politics in a changing international economic system, are not the unilateral responsibility of the United States. But because the United States is the leader of the capitalist world, its policies exacerbate the underlying dangers. The warfare state generates new forms of insecurity. The United States cannot long survive with it, but its system of corporate capitalism seems unable to live without it.

As these constraints accumulate, and some come near to being contradictions, the political economy of corporate capitalism approaches a condition of paralysis. Each effort to remedy one problem within the limits allowed by the prevailing system threatens to magnify a dislocation somewhere else. The resulting binds are manifested in the deterioration of the family, the near collapse of cities, the decay of the natural environment, the continuing struggle by workers for economic security, and the increasing number of citizens classified as welfare recipients. Politically these binds are reflected in the expansion of tax rates, in the decline in utility of state services, in the deadly growth of the warfare-welfare state, in the explosive emotions attaching to marginal and symbolic issues such as "law and order," busing, affirmative action, welfare fraud, abortion, and in the general erosion in public support for liberal ideology. The paralyzed economy brings with it doubts about the performance and legitimacy of the welfare state.

The Welfare State

The welfare state, as the legitimate agency through which collective problems are supposed to be resolved by public means, is the recipient of pressures generated by the corporate sector. It is held responsible for resolving these problems, but the limited tools legitimately available to it ensure that each attempted solution will be only partly successful in the short run while tending to create new limits to viable state action in the future.

Though the term welfare state reflects a liberal commitment to public policies that enhance the material welfare of the working class and underclass by redistributing income from the rich to the poor, in fact the bias of the welfare state moves in a different direction. Its actual priorities fit the following pattern:

1. Because corporate production is social and worldwide in nature, it requires massive support from the state in the form of investments and subsidies to support its activities.

2. Because corporate production is mobilized in the interests of private profit, it generates costly side effects that the state must cope with in some way.

3. Because companies in the market sector are caught in a competitive squeeze and disadvantaged through terms of trade with companies in the corporate sector, the state is also called upon to provide them with subsidies and protection.

4. Workers in the corporate sector, marginal employees in the market sector, and other various outcasts, victimized by social atomization, low supply of jobs, and high costs of living, call upon the state to help them. The public responses to these pleas give the welfare state its name, while accounting for only a small part of its activities.

Spending by all levels of government (see Table 6-1) reflects the impressive expansion of the welfare state. Total expenditures were $2 billion in 1902 and $461 billion by 1974; they moved from under 8 percent of the Gross National Product in the first year to 33 percent by 1974. To understand the direction in which benefits from these expenditures flow, consider first those that benefit corporate owners, affluent consumers, and technical-professional workers most directly.

Military expenditures promote profits for a range of private corporations. They generate research findings available to corporations, provide jobs primarily for highly trained technicians (a large percentage of engineers, physicists, airplane mechanics, and so on, are employed by the defense economy), and provide protection for cor-

TABLE 6-1. **Spending by All Levels of Government, 1902–1974**

Year	Billions of Dollars	Percent of GNP
1902	1.7	7.7
1913	3.2	8.2
1922	9.3	12.5
1929	10.3	10.0
1934	12.9	19.8
1939	17.6	19.4
1944	103.0	49.1
1949	59.1	23.0
1954	96.7	26.5
1959	131.0	27.1
1964	175.4	27.7
1969	290.1	31.2
1974	460.9	33.0

Source: 1902, 1913, and 1922 are from Thomas A. Dye, Understanding Public Policy (Englewood Cliffs, N.J.: Prentice Hall, 1972), p. 186. 1929–1974 are calculated from tables in Economic Report of the President, 1971 and 1975.

porate investments in foreign countries. These expenditures also provide employment for working-class soldiers who might otherwise be unemployed or marginally employed, diminishing thereby the flow of state expenditures to welfare and unemployment insurance. Expenditures for public higher education subsidize the education of children from middle- and upper-income families. Since all citizens are taxed to support these programs, and since a significantly smaller proportion of low-income children attend college (see Table 6-2) low-income taxpayers in the effect subsidize the education of higher-income students.

Heavy government expenditures for highways, airports, housing, technical training of corporate employees, and credit guarantees subsidize corporate activities and the activities of middle- and high-income families. For the poor do not use interstate highways for vacation, recreation, and business trips; they seldom travel by airplane; and public housing programs rarely reach them. Tax subsidies in the form of favored treatment by the individual states and localities to attract business, tax deductions for mortgage interest rates, and other forms of tax itemization, primarily benefit businesses

TABLE 6-2.   College Attendance in 1967 of High School Graduates by Family Income

Family Income	Percent Who Did Not Attend College	Percent Who Did Attend College
Total	53.1	46.9
Under $3000	80.2	19.8
$3000–$3999	67.7	32.3
$4000–$5999	63.1	36.9
$6000–$7499	58.9	41.1
$7500–$9999	49.0	51.0
$10,000–$14,999	38.7	61.3
$15,000 and over	13.3	86.7

Source: United States Bureau of the Census, *Current Population Report*, Series P-20, No. 185 (July 11, 1969), p. 6.

and affluent consumers. Farm subsidy programs go primarily to the wealthiest farmers, the richest 19 percent receiving about 63 percent of the benefits and the poorest 63 percent getting about 9 percent.[6]

Even the social security system, while indispensable to old people at present, is not really class-redistributive in its effects. Funded by a regressive tax, it represents a redistribution across generations *within* the working class rather than between the working and owning classes. Or consider the huge expenditures at all levels of government for police and surveillance activity. The expenditures proliferate as the welfare state fails to cope with the social malaise and economic insecurity that corporate capitalism produces among the underclass. The services primarily benefit the middle and upper classes, whose security would otherwise be threatened; though certainly, insofar as no alternatives are available, members of the underclass are grateful for the marginal increase in security these forces provide for them.

There are expenditures, required largely because of defects in the employment-income system of corporate capitalism, that do fit the liberal idealization of the welfare state. Such relief and welfare programs are concentrated in the major cities, where approximately one out of every seven or eight residents receives welfare; among blacks, who make up a large proportion of the underclass; and among the disabled of various sorts. These programs are generally maintained at levels low enough to ensure that no competition will exist between the benefit levels and the lowest paying jobs in the market sector. Aid to Families of Dependent Children, aid to the aged, the disabled, and the blind are indispensable to the recipients, but all these payments combined constitute no more than 10 percent of total government expenditures at all levels.[7] The payments do relieve some of the worst hardships of those in the greatest need; they do contribute to the political quiescence of the client groups; but when total government expenditures are considered, they do not amount to a redistribution by government from the rich to the poor.

Governments at all levels—local, state, and federal—must somehow finance warfare-welfare state expenditures. Theoretically, they can finance them through profits earned from publicly owned productive enterprises, deficit spending through debt creation, or taxation of various sorts. But the first route is illegitimate in the welfare state, and deficit spending, available only to the federal government, is limited by the tendency of such deficits to fuel inflation. As a result the individual state and local governments, where the relief and welfare budgets are concentrated, depend almost entirely on taxes to finance these expenditures, and the national government also depends on them to a great extent. As we saw in Chapter 3, when all taxes are included, such as sales, excise, property, state income, national income, inheritance, and corporate, the effect of the tax system is to maintain inequality. The total result we can now see, of the tax-expenditure system in the welfare state is a nonredistributive tax system used to finance government programs biased toward corporate owners and affluent consumers.

The crisis of the welfare state has several dimensions. We first list several of them and then ask, To what extent is this crisis a necessary feature of our system of corporate capitalism?

1. As the demands for public expenditures have escalated, taxpayers have been caught in the squeeze. Their taxes at all levels of government are rising while the quality of services, especially in urban areas, is declining.

2. As the state has come to play an increasingly important role in the economy, the number and variety of public-sector workers has increased. As James O'Connor, the political economist who has explored this dimension of the welfare state crisis most thoroughly, notes:

The United States federal government employs about 2.5 million civilian workers in eighty departments and agencies and nearly 4 million in the armed forces, and total state and local government employment is roughly 8.5 million. . . . In addition to the 11 million workers employed directly by the state, there are countless wage and salary earners—perhaps as many as 25 to 30 million—who are employed by private capital dependent in whole or in part on state contracts and facilities.[8]

The size and shape of the public sector creates limits to public budgetary policy. For while public-sector workers strive to match the income levels of similarly trained workers in the corporate sector, the very nature of their work in teaching, social work, research, program administration, and so on, makes it unlikely that they can achieve similar productivity gains. Thus as they gain higher wages, they help to generate inflation. The inflation increases the costly government programs and further limits the range of policies the state can employ to manage the business cycle or to finance its own expenditures.

3. During periods of stagflation, individual state and local governments, which carry the greatest burden of welfare and relief payments, are trapped in a serious bind. They cannot depend on deficit financing. Increased unemployment magnifies the size of welfare budgets while it decreases the size of tax revenue. Tax increases needed to meet these costs are bitterly resisted by citizens already injured by inflationary spirals and by business interests that demand a favorable investment climate in order to increase production and employment levels. State and local governments are then under intense pressure to cut back welfare and other public programs at exactly the time the programs are the most needed.

4. Since the state is accountable to public constituencies while private producers are not, citizens tend to blame the state for failing to keep the economy on an even keel. For example, 48 percent of the population in 1974 held the government responsible for inflation, while only 16 percent traced inflation to business activity. Interestingly, 51 percent of manual, clerical, and sales workers placed primary responsibility for inflation on the government.[9] Most people also blame high tax levels on inefficiency in government more than on imperatives imposed upon the state by the costs of corporate capitalism. And since the federal government in 1946 committed itself to the goal of full employment, it is widely assumed that the state could, if it were more efficient and energetic, sustain full employment, low inflation, and lower taxes within the current system of political economy. But it cannot.

The state is the legitimate forum of accountability and it is thereby looked to for redress and assistance when people are threatened by inflation, unemployment, environmental destruction, and crime. But it lacks the resources to deal effectively with the dislocations of corporate capitalism and to meet the public expectations it has helped to create. As its programs and costs accumulate, as its ineffectiveness becomes increasingly apparent, citizens respond by losing confidence in the government institutions through which welfare state programs are processed. Thus in a 1975 Harris Poll only 13 percent of the population expressed confidence in Congress, 13 percent in the executive branch of the federal government, 16 percent in state government, and 13 percent in local government.[10]

This loss of confidence represents a distrust of politicians, a cynicism about corruption and graft in government, and growing doubts about the ability of government to resolve pressing economic problems. The form it takes, though, is very often misplaced. Some believe that the market system could operate justly and efficiently if only the state would retreat to a position of benign neglect; they fail to see that the expanded state role has in fact been necessary to maintain the system of corporate capitalism. In the eyes of others, changes in public personnel and in particular programs within the framework of corporate capitalism would appear to be sufficient. They, too, fail to see that the state ignores so many collective needs in large part, at least, because it too is trapped within the binds of corporate capitalism. The decline in public confidence in the welfare state, then, tends to misinterpret the real crisis of performance in the entire system of political economy. The welfare state becomes the scapegoat for problems that are in fact more deeply anchored in the very terms of relations between the state and the economy in the political economy of corporate capitalism. And this gap between public perception and reality carries dangerous political implications.

A key assumption embedded in the above argument deserves further attention: Does the crisis in the performance and legitimacy of the welfare state reflect the political ability of corporate elites to prevail over liberals and populists in setting the actual agenda of public policy, or does it reflect certain structural imperatives of corporate capitalism that require such a tax–expenditure agenda no matter which groups have privileged access to public officials? Theorists such as C. Wright Mills and Ralph Miliband tend toward the former interpretation, and the latter is more congenial to Paul Sweezy and French Marxists like Louis Althusser and Nicos Poulantzas.[11] The issues were clearly laid out in a debate between Miliband and Poulantzas.

Poulantzas criticizes theories of the capitalist state that seek to show that government-administrative elites are primarily of upper-class background and are continuously responsive to pressures by members of this same class:

> The relation between the bourgeois class and the state is an objective relation. . . . Indeed, in the case of the capitalist state, one can go further: It can be said that the capitalist state best serves the interests of the capitalist class only when members of this class do not participate directly in the state apparatus, this is to say, when the ruling class is not the politically governing class. [12]

Ralph Miliband, whose own study of the state moved Poulantzas to make those criticisms, takes issue with the emphasis in Poulantzas's study:

> What his exclusive stress on "objective relations" suggests is that what the state does is in every particular and at all times wholly determined by these "objective relations": in other words, that the structural constraints of the system are so absolutely compelling as to turn those who run the state into the merest functionaries and executants of policies imposed upon them by "the system". . . . The state elite is involved in a far more complex relationship with "the system" . . . than Poulantzas' scheme allows. . . . [13]

In our view, Poulantzas, if in an exaggerated form, points to tendencies in the relation between the welfare state and corporate capitalism that American liberals and radicals have too often ignored. Two tendencies are at work within corporate capitalism, each moving in a different time frame but combining at strategic junctures to impose powerful constraints on state action.

First, over the longer run, as structural constraints proliferate and some come near to being contradictions, the welfare state must respond within a narrow range of policy options to keep the system afloat. For example, it cannot significantly reduce inequality; it cannot introduce a highly progressive tax system; it must maintain a large military structure; it cannot introduce meaningful work reform; it must, in times of economic difficulty, favor incentives to investors while imposing constraints on marginal workers in the economy; it cannot plan effectively enough to restore the integrity of crumbling urban areas, but it can expand police, surveillance, and prison facilities in an effort to maintain order there; it cannot forestall the erosion of family and community ties, but can only provide marginal material support to the oldest and youngest victims of this erosion. These broad limits apply whether liberals or business conservatives are in office, and whether the ideological pendulum has swung toward or away from "big business."

Second, within these larger limits, welfare state options fluctuate with the ebb and flow of the business cycle. When the business cycle is at a peak—when investment, production, consumption, and employment are at high levels—*power struggles* between liberals and conservatives in local, state, and national governments exert an important influence over policy outcomes. Liberals typically press to spend a larger portion of revenues on welfare, health, insurance, and education. These are programs benefiting (in order) middle- and lower-income citizens and the working and nonworking poor. Business conservatives press to concentrate public subsidies in areas of more direct benefit to corporate owners, small businesses, and affluent consumers. Federal and individual state legislatures provide the arenas in which these conflicts are resolved; interest group maneuvering and log-rolling strategies are important determinants of the outcomes.

When the business cycle moves into a contractionary phase, though, and particularly when the contraction includes the stagflation of recent years, the options available to the welfare state are very limited whether its incumbent officers are liberal or conservative in ideology. These limits are most sharply exposed at the level of individual state governments. Thus in the middle 1970s liberal governors such as Dukakis in Massachusetts, Grasso in Connecticut, Carey in New York, and Brown in California were forced to go against their own ideological inclinations. Faced with declining revenues, growing expenditures for welfare, and inflated prices for state services, each gave high priority to welfare cuts while trying to retain other programs favorable to corporate and financial investors. And when increased taxes became necessary, they came mostly out of the pockets of average taxpayers already hit by inflation, high tax rates, and the threat of unemployment.

In a private corporate economy, corporate owners must be given *incentives* to invest, produce, and employ. Otherwise they might reduce investments; they might relocate in another state inside the United States; or they might divert a portion of their investments and plant to another country with a more favorable business climate. The marginal members of society—the unemployed and the underemployed, the old and the indigent, the unorganized workers—can be *coerced* to work for less, to accept higher prices, to pay higher taxes, and to face heightened job insecurity. Liberal governors and legislators may not like the mix of tools available to them, but when the economic crunch is on, they apply the carrot to privileged constituencies and the stick to the marginal clients.

The welfare state operates within a set of structural constraints, sometimes rather loosely defined, sometimes rigidly operative. The crisis in performance and legitimacy of the welfare state reflects its inability to meet the needs of people within those constraints. And the crisis is accentuated by the fact that liberal politicians and publicists have repeatedly made promises in the name of the welfare state that it cannot keep.

The Erosion of Liberalism

The crisis of the welfare state does not mean that it will collapse of its own weight. Rather, several possibilities remain open:

1. The state might muddle through for an indefinite period, holding the system together by repression for some, the promise of escape and advancement for others, and protection for the most privileged. But lost in the muddle would be the poor, the needs of cities, the environment, the inflation squeeze on low- and middle-income employees, and the malaise of the workers.

2. An emergent proto-fascist response might protect the welfare state and the corporate system. Those shuffled out of the system, and those who identify with them, would be subject to increasing repression and intimidation, while corporate elites and workers in the corporate system would coalesce in opposition to the outcasts and the critics.

3. As the crisis deepens, and as the United States continues to depend on foreign markets, labor, and resources in an increasingly hostile world, one or more wars might be launched against foreign adversaries. Internal unity against foreign threats would be sought at the risk of nuclear destruction or the return to universal barbarism.

4. The failures and criticisms of the welfare state could generate a viable movement toward a socialist system. This would be the most rational response, but it is also one full of risks and pitfalls. These risks are anchored partly in the political hostility that socialist movements receive in American society and partly in the insufficient development of socialist theory itself.

What the welfare state of today cannot do is to deliver on the promises of contemporary liberalism. As an ideology supporting the economic and social needs of the working class and the underclass within corporate capitalism, liberalism is increasingly vulnerable. Its vulnerability flows not so much from the widely perceived gap between the rhetoric of liberals seeking office and their actual intentions; rather, the liberal ideology defeats itself in the very process of trying to fulfill its most humane objectives through the welfare state. In the new situation, unless liberals move to the left they will be forced increasingly by events to slide to the right.[14]

Liberals accept the system of production for private profit while expecting the welfare state to support the corporate structure, to absorb the social costs of production for profit, and to rectify the injustices done to those shuffled out of the production system. Within that framework, liberals pose a range of state programs. We have already criticized liberal programs for management of the business cycle (Keynesianism), reduction in inequality (progressive taxation), ecological restoration (the economics of environmental management), and the marginal reform of work life (reordering trade union priorities). But other implications of these programs, when they are considered as a package, still need to be examined.

First, success in any area is closely connected to success in the others. And a crucial precondition for all the others is persistent success in regulating the business cycle through Keynesian tools while maintaining high rates of economic growth. Without success here, the tax base required for the other programs cannot be created. Without that base neither a reduction in inequality through progressive taxation nor the increased taxes and consumer costs required for environmental management can hope to gain voluntary constituency assent. Without a large social dividend created by an expanded tax base, public programs in health care, transportation, urban restoration, and welfare will not grow substantially. Given the systemic constraints accepted by liberals, then, it is easy to see why liberals in office typically give economic growth the highest priority and often support enthusiastically tax and subsidy incentives to business as the appropriate means to promote that growth. The liberal consistently supports business priorities today in the hope of creating space tomorrow for cherished liberal programs. That is why Walter Heller, a liberal Keynesian economist in the Kennedy administration, was so bullish after that administration had successfully encouraged economic growth through a cut in business taxes. "When the cost of fulfilling a people's aspirations," he said, "can be met out of a growing horn of plenty, ideological roadblocks melt away, and consensus replaces conflict."[15]

But the obverse is also true. When the policies spurring economic growth have adverse side effects like inflation, environmental deterioration, overexpansion of debt, an international arms race, unemployment, and withdrawal by the affluent from the urban centers, the state will lack the resources and will to cope with these consequences when the next downturn occurs. When production for profit requires extensive inequality and alienating work, the state will refuse to tamper with these institutions. When the horn of plenty turns into a squeezed accordion as the business cycle slides into its contractionary phase, ideological roadblocks will reappear and consensus will be replaced by class conflict and coercion. Liberals, refusing to acknowledge these structural limits to the liberal agenda, repeatedly justify short-run sacrifices by the subordinate classes in the form of unemployment, wage restraints, and welfare cuts while looking ahead to the next boom for a climate more favorable to the expansion of the welfare state. If radicals, as their critics say, continually tilt at the proverbial windmill, liberals remain content to ride its blade round and round.

But the poverty of liberalism assumes other dimensions as well. By making public promises in the name of the welfare state, liberals encourage unemployed workers, victims of inflation, paralyzed urban residents, and welfare recipients to support policies that will not securely promote their needs over the long run. The disappointed constituencies then blame the state for its failure to solve problems that are in fact outside its capability in the prevailing system of political economy. Expanding the size and role of the welfare state, encouraging its movement into unprofitable areas of public need while reserving profitable enterprises for the private sector, liberalism contributes to the fiscal crisis of the state. It thus plays into the hands of business conservatives who claim persistently that the state is inherently unable to produce goods and services efficiently; and it generates public expectations that cannot be met effectively within the established system. Liberalism, in these ways, accentuates a crisis anchored in the irrational relation between the welfare state and the corporate economy while it diverts the affected constituencies from ideological alternatives that might connect their troubles more closely to the irrational relation itself.

Liberals and their major ideological adversaries—business conservatives—agree on one important premise: When things go wrong the state is primarily responsible. Thus when things do go wrong—when liberal programs fail, when citizens are caught in a tax-inflation squeeze, when the unemployed and the unemployable face welfare cuts, when public sector employees face pay cuts—the state rather than the entire political economy of corporate capitalism is held responsible by liberal and conservative constituencies. In a political debate where the system of political economy is accepted by both parties, the accumulation of economic dislocations will most surely undermine the position of those who have advanced positive programs to remedy these defects. Since liberalism celebrates the welfare state, the crisis of the welfare state means the erosion of liberal constituencies.

It is clear that most Americans today are unwilling to call themselves liberals. Thus in 1973, 37 percent labeled themselves conservative, 37 percent middle of the road, and only 24 percent liberal.[16] These figures underplay both the resilience in electoral support for moderately liberal candidates and the intense resentment felt by many against liberal welfare and tax programs. The fall in electoral support for liberalism would be greater yet if there were viable options open to the disaffected. But most working Americans detect the class bias in the business conservatism of the Republican party, and few can move easily or comfortably in that direction, even though that is the only legitimate move available within the established electoral system. With nowhere else to go, the hostility to liberalism initially finds expression in spontaneous, unorganized ways—as in support for George Wallace, in the growing number of independent voters, in tax revolts at the lower levels of government, in minority support for the idea of a new party on the right, or in an uneasy withdrawal from the political arena altogether.

The present period, defined politically, is one of unrest, uncertainty, and ambivalence in the subordinate classes. Trapped within the limited electoral options available, distressed citizens might eventually move in surprising directions. This is a time fraught with danger as the manifest failures of the welfare state threaten to feed the forces of repression. It is also a time in which the radical's comprehension of the political economy of corporate capitalism might introduce new pressures into the old contests and coalitions. It is a time when the socialist agenda can aspire to a wider audience than it has yet received.

The Socialist Idea

There is no heaven on earth. Every system of political economy in a complex society will generate a range of limits and constraints. What is true of corporate capitalism is true, in its own way, of socialism too. The fact that corporate capitalism forces workers to struggle for security, the fact that it generates extremes of opulence and poverty, environmental degradation, militarism, and degrading forms of work—these provide sufficient reason to explore the promise of other systems. But the injustices and irrationalities of corporate capitalism are not themselves sufficient to justify any particular alternative. While our primary purpose in this text has been to establish the case for exploring socialist alternatives, we will close with a few comments about the terrain to be explored.

The hope of socialism is twofold: to regulate production of goods and services in the interests of human need and equality rather than private profit and to reduce or eliminate the exploitation and domination of some over others. Democratic socialism hopes to promote these ends by *politicizing* a process of planning and producing that is already social in form and consequence. It seeks to insert public control and accountability into production relations themselves.

But the ideal of socialism contains within itself a potential contradiction. The planning system required to promote rational production might also be employed to repress and intimidate segments of the population. The means required to promote equality may also diminish freedom. This is the fear that leads many liberals and radicals who accept criticisms of corporate capitalism to shy away from the socialist idea itself.

Historical experience with socialism is quite limited. Advanced industrial societies have not yet introduced it, and industrializing and nonindustrial systems have introduced variants under the most adverse circumstances. There is, then, no historical experience closely applicable to the United States as an advanced industrial society. Optimistic or pessimistic extrapolations from the experience of other countries must therefore be viewed with caution.

Nonetheless, sociologist Frank Parkin's exploration of the promise and problems of socialist countries in the Soviet orbit deserves to be taken seriously. First, the promise. In these systems, says Parkin, since economic burdens and benefits are distributed *transparently* through a political process rather than *opaquely* through a market mechanism, economic inequality is notably reduced (including the reduction of unemployment, the expansion of public over private goods and services, and a narrowing of income differentials):

> *Thus, one of the features of a stratification order based primarily on the market is that the allocation of rewards is generally*

not in the hands of an easily identifiable and political bounded
social group. . . . This is especially so with respect to class
perceptions of inequality. . . . In a command system, on the
other hand, distribution is primarily decided on the basis of
direct political agency. . . . In other words, the source of
inequality is primarily political, and by this token, more readily
controlled by legislative fiat.[17]

But there is another side to state control of production and
distribution. The central coordination required to rationalize the
system of production and to reduce inequality increases the state's
resources and incentive to stifle political dissent. Parkin, writing with
socialist aspirations, is blunt about his perceptions and fears in this
regard:

Egalitarianism seems to require a political system in which the
state is able continually to hold in check those social and
occupational groups which by virtue of their skills or education
or personal attributes might otherwise attempt to stake claims
to a disproportionate share of society's rewards. The most
effective way of holding such groups in check is by denying
them the right to organize politically . . . to undermine social
equality.[18]

Parkin squarely confronts the sorest spots in socialist theory and
in established socialist practice. His fears echo the more stark assertion by Milton Friedman noted in Chapter 1—that there is complete,
uneliminable antagonism between socialism and freedom. Let us,
though, consider various aspects of this issue in an American context.

1. The inability of the welfare state to cope with poverty and
racism, to reverse the trend toward urban collapse, to create meaningful careers for new generations, to reduce the hostility of the
Third World to the United States—all these failures encourage it to
expand police, military, and surveillance forces at home and abroad.
If it cannot cope with the causes of crime and terrorism, it does have
the resources and public support needed to respond repressively to
criminals, terrorists, and their actual or purported sympathizers. The
mode of response, in ways that hardly need elaboration to the contemporary newspaper reader, undermine freedom of assembly, pri-
vacy, and dissent. The threat to freedom emerges inside the welfare
state as well as inside the socialist state.[19]

2. A certain range of freedom—the freedom to invest for private profit, to exploit the labor of others, to secure privileges denied to others—must be reduced or eliminated in any socialist society. But the corollary is true in corporate capitalism as well: The freedom of workers to control the work process, to engage in unalienating work, and to gain the benefits of job security are all structurally limited. There are thus different limits set by the pursuit of different ends in each system, and it would be quite misleading to call one set an infringement upon liberties while avoiding that assertion with respect to the other.

3. The proliferating dislocations of corporate capitalism have already generated, and will increasingly require, *expansion in capitalist planning,* that is in planning to spur economic growth by securing increasing profits for owners. Recent calls for expanded planning by such luminaries as industrialist Henry Ford, the editors of the *New York Times*, John Kenneth Galbraith, the Nobel Prize economist Wassily Leontieff, and Felix G. Rohayton, the financial advisor to Henry Jackson, all testify to the likely acceleration of this contemporary trend. Rohayton, for instance, calls for a new Reconstruction Finance Corporation that would spur economic growth by subsidizing corporate investment into crucial areas. He observes:

> There can be no denying that such an organization can be perceived as a first step toward state planning of the economy. Yet the time may have come for a public debate on this subject. . . . The premise that under [existing] circumstances, the country has to husband its resources more carefully, allocate them more prudently, and match its financial capabilities with its social priorities would appear to be worth considering. What many will call state planning would, to the average family, be no more than prudent budgeting.[20]

Set in this context the problem of freedom is increasingly seen as a problem for industrial society as such. The question is not, Should we have planning? but, What sort of planning? Subject to what modes of political accountability? Inspired by what social purposes? Our own judgment is that the ideal of social planning must be combined with public ownership of corporate enterprises, retention of a market sector that includes publishing and journal enterprises, work reform, and enhanced worker participation in industrial decision making. That combination, we suspect, carries the greatest promise for protecting citizen dissent while orienting the production system more closely to the needs of all citizens.[21]

Socialism, as an ideal, is outside the range of established ideological debate in America. This exclusion partly accounts for the failure of radicals to explore closely the problem of maintaining freedom within a socialist polity. It is imperative now, though, that this deficiency in socialist thought be remedied. Only then can the left combine its critical analysis with an affirmative agenda, can it provide new alternatives to liberals who threaten to slide to the right, can it exert effective pressure on those owners and public officials quite willing to assert that any industrial society must impose low wages, job insecurity, authoritarian modes of work, high costs of living, and escalating taxes on vast numbers of its citizens.

To dissect the irrationalities of corporate capitalism, the crisis of the welfare state, and the erosion of liberal ideology is to make the exploration of democratic socialism a matter of the highest priority for those committed to a more humane social order.

NOTES

1. By "state" we mean a nation-state rather than a state government such as Massachusetts or Ohio, unless otherwise specified or clear from context.
2. When we speak of structural constraints, we do not usually refer to constraints in *all* capitalist countries but to those operative in the United States system of corporate capitalism. There are connections, though. For example, where would the other capitalist countries be without our military shield? Where would many of them be without our economic penetration and our role in redevelopment after World War II? The unique features in our system—features we have developed highly—still affect the world capitalist system, even if other capitalist countries have not found it necessary to incorporate them. They have not, in part at least, because we have. This is a consideration when asked, Why doesn't Germany have X or Sweden Y if those are features of corporate capitalism (not just happenstances) in America?
3. The long-range employment effect of corporate movement abroad is controversial. Some argue a net loss in jobs is the result; others contend that job opportunities created in United States multinational corporate headquarters and by repatriated profits are greater than job losses. It is certain that the greater freedom of capital to move gives management a powerful lever in labor negotiations. For a survey of recent literature on the subject, see Richard J. Barnet and Ronald E. Muller, *Global Reach: The Power of Multinational Corporations* (New York: Simon and Schuster, 1975), ch. 11.

4. We are not arguing against women's right to work, just as our critique of welfare does not question the rights of those currently in the status of welfare recipients. The point is that the most effective form the grievances of dissident or oppressed minorities can assume in the established system either contributes to problems for them elsewhere or projects new burdens on other minorities.

5. In 1974 the United States exported $8 billion in arms. Between 1963 and 1973 the United States was responsible for 51 percent and the USSR for 27 percent of world military exports. See *World Arms Trade* (Bureau of Public Affairs, Department of State, July 1975).

6. Taylor Branch, "The Screwing of the Average Man: Who Gets the $63 Billion?" *Washington Monthly* (March 1972), p. 64.

7. See Richard C. Edwards, "Who Fares Well in the Welfare State," in *The Capitalist System*, ed. Richard C. Edwards, Michael Reich and Thomas E. Weisskopf (Englewood Cliffs, N.J.: Prentice Hall, 1972), pp. 244–251, and Edward S. Greenberg, *Serving the Few: Corporate Capitalism and the Bias of Government Policy* (New York: Wiley, 1974), pp. 214–226.

8. *The Corporations and the State* (New York: Harper and Row, 1974), pp. 105, 106.

9. *Gallup Opinion Index* (September 1974), p. 31.

10. Reported in the *Boston Globe*, July 9, 1975.

11. See Mills, *The Power Elite* (New York: Oxford University Press, 1959); Miliband, *The State in Capitalist Society* (New York: Basic Books, 1969); Sweezy, *The Theory of Capitalist Development* (New York: Monthly Review Press, 1968); and Althusser, *For Marx* (New York: Vintage Books, 1969).

12. "The Problem of the Capitalist State," in *Ideology in Social Science*, ed. Robin Blackburn (New York: Vintage Books, 1973), pp. 245, 246.

13. "Reply to Nicos Poulantzas," Ibid., pp. 258–259.

14. We focus on liberal economic programs, not on the liberal commitments to dissent and free assembly. But these latter ideals depend to a great extent upon success in promoting the liberal economic agenda within the welfare state.

15. *New Dimensions of Political Economy* (Cambridge: Harvard University Press, 1967), p. 12.

16. Louis Harris, *The Anguish of Change* (New York: Norton, 1973), p. 249.

17. *Class Inequality and Political Order* (New York: Praeger, 1971), pp. 160–161, 168.

18. Ibid., p. 183.

19. For a good recent history of such tendencies in America, see Alan Wolfe, *The Seamy Side of Democracy* (New York: McKay, 1973).

20. "A New RFC Is Proposed for Business," *New York Times*, December 1, 1974.

21. The problem of making socialist planning consistent with individual freedom is perhaps the crucial issue in socialist thought. An excellent beginning is made by Paul Ricoeur, "The Political Paradox," in *Existential Phenomenology and Political Theory*, ed. Hwa Yol Tung (Chicago: Regnery, 1972), pp. 337–367.

Index